Covenant and Community

Covenant and Community
Our Role as the Image of God

Doug P. Baker

WIPF & STOCK · Eugene, Oregon

COVENANT AND COMMUNITY
Our Role as the Image of God

Copyright © 2008 Doug P. Baker. All rights reserved. Except for brief quotations in critical publications or reviews, no part of this book may be reproduced in any manner without prior written permission from the publisher. Write: Permissions, Wipf & Stock Publishers, 199 W. 8th Ave., Suite 3, Eugene, OR 97401.

ISBN 13: 978-1-55635-203-4

Manufactured in the U.S.A.

*To the memory of Tim Eekhoff
who wept for me long before God granted me
tears to weep for my own sin.*

*Tim, your tears for me filled up
what was still lacking in the sufferings of Christ.
In my memory of you I see a hint
of what the fulfillment of God's image will be.*

Contents

Preface / ix

Abbreviations / xiii

1. Five Questions / 1
2. Let Us Make / 16
3. Make, Create, and Form / 24
4. Adam / 41
5. In the Role of God's Image / 56
6. God's Self-Revelation / 71
7. The Trinity / 80
8. Covenant / 95
9. God's Image After the Fall / 114
10. Jesus, God's Express Image / 129

Bibliography / 141

Preface

It is often easier to accept and comprehend each step along a path if we know at the outset what our destination is to be. To that end I offer this short version of the book's main thrust.

- God's image, as used in Genesis 1:26, has nothing to do with the blueprint of how we were made, and even less to do with our abilities, desires, or even our original purity. God's image was not lost at the Fall, because we never had it to begin with. God's image was not "in" us. Rather, we were made "in the role of the Trinity's image and for the purpose of their likeness." The words "our image" describe not us but our intended function in creation. This is our telos, the end toward which we were made. Furthermore, we are expected to fulfill this function, and failure to do so is sin.

- God's image will ultimately be manifest not primarily in individuals but in humanity as a whole, specifically in the community of the saints. This group will be united, without diminishing but rather fulfilling the individuality of its members, in a union imaging the three-who-are-one union of the Godhead.

- God will fulfill what he proposed at our creation; he will complete the work of seeing his image displayed through us. His image is the eschatological end toward which the entire universe was created, toward which God sent Satan into the garden, toward which Jesus was sacrificed. This vast history was designed by the Father to bring glory to his beloved Son.

- In the end, for God's image to be complete, we must be entwined into the intimate fellowship of the Trinity and bound together with Jesus as his bride; we will become family members with the God-family. Only then will we be able finally to fulfill our role as humans.

Thus the reader knows at the outset where this book will end. Those four points sum up the substance of the following pages; all the rest is details.

The details will, however, encompass a vast domain: creation, covenants between God and humanity, human purpose, marriage, parenthood, human destiny, life, death and hell, Jesus on the cross, future glory, sin and righteousness, and many other topics of concern not only to theologians but also to every child of Adam and Eve. In fact, the idea of being made to express God's image and experience his likeness will be seen to touch on every possible aspect of human life and even human death. I have come to believe that these are among the most all-encompassing four words in the entire Bible; they are equal in weight and scope to other massive phrases, such as "Because I live, you will live also" or "God is love." In them God proposed not only that we be made, but also to what end we were to be made, and he included his Son and his Spirit in the work; it was to be a team effort.

The first half of *Covenant and Community* is dedicated to probing four words that Moses wrote in Genesis 1:26, which are generally rendered into English as something like, "Let us make man in our image and according to our likeness." We can see already that what Moses said in four words has taken a dozen to translate, and it will take more than a few more to come to grips with their import.

The second half of the book considers a few of the many implications of the doctrine that emerge from our exegesis. There we ask such questions as "How does this doctrine of God's image impact our understanding of sin, righteousness, and Jesus' atonement?" The body of questions examined is necessarily limited and the treatment of each is brief. It has been possible here merely to touch on a few key areas of intersection, delving into none deeply and passing by others altogether. Nonetheless, those that are considered indicate both the breadth and depth of impact that a proper understanding of our role in this universe ought to have on our understanding of ourselves as creatures and on our understanding of the special relationship into which we have been created. It is my conviction that, were someone to undertake the task, the whole of systematic theology could be advanced by re-evaluating all aspects within it in the expectation that all theological understanding must spring from three great truths: the Trinity, covenant, and God's image. That work will wait.

Though only a few topics can be treated in these pages, it is hoped that the reader will be able to extrapolate attitudes and lifestyles in keeping with the doctrines discussed. Little is done, however, by way of application in this present text. Application is left to the Christian reader and the pastor.

I wish to thank a few of those who have been invaluable in the preparation of this present work: John Armstrong, who published an earlier article on God's image in *Reformation and Revival Journal* of which this present book is an expansion; Patrick Kuhlman, pastor of Trinity Lutheran Church, Ellettsville, Indiana, for his careful reading and critiquing in a very early form of the main ideas presented; Dennis Fisher, whose critique early on helped clarify the thesis which is pursued; Rick Stringfellow, whose computer help and gifts were in daily use as I worked on the manuscript; Charles Taber, whose thoughtful critique was invaluable for making the final revisions; Dwight P. Baker and Lois I. Baker, my parents, who spent uncounted hours correcting my spelling, punctuation, style, and grammar; Noelle, Hannah, Lillyanna, and Hope Malan, my daughters, who cheered me on when I most needed it. To these and many others who commented on and made suggestions concerning the manuscript, I am deeply aware of my debt. It goes without saying that none of the above are responsible for any errors or foolish statements in the following pages; the errors represent places where I stubbornly refused to heed the advice of wiser minds. Forgive me.

Abbreviations

CEV	Contemporary English Version
ESV	English Standard Version
JPS	*Hebrew-English Tanakh*
KJV	King James or Authorized Version
NASB	New American Standard Bible
NET	New English Translation NET Bible
NIV	New International Version
NLT	New Living Translation
NRSV	New Revised Standard Version
TDNT	*Theological Dictionary of the New Testament*

1

Five Questions

DAVID LOOKED about at the greasy people, smelling of sweat and sheep and blood, milling around him and jostling each other at the Tabernacle of the Lord. He saw them laughing and calling out, kneeling in prayer and singing together; he saw the cripples at the gate, the poor with their pigeons, and the wealthy with their colorful robes. He saw them all and he saw himself in all the filthiness of his own heart, a man who had been taken from the fields where he had slept with the sheep, who had been elevated by the creator of the universe to be a king and to sleep in stately rooms. He looked around at the crowd and he asked God the eternal question, "What is man? What am I? Why would the creator of the universe care about us, about me?"

David's question, so famously asked in Psalm 8, has been ringing in every human soul ever since we hid in the bushes from the sound of God's approach. We may have the option of ignoring the question's answer, but we do not have the ability not to ask it. Every human senses the ownership and rulership of a creator, as Paul takes pains to make clear in the opening chapters of his letter to the Romans, and we all sense our own littleness compared not only with the vast creation but much more when we regard ourselves sitting on the lap of an even greater Creator. In such musings we all, whether informed by Scriptures or not, ask similar questions to those asked by David:

> When I behold Your heavens, the work of Your fingers,
>> the moon and stars that You set in place,
>> what is man that You have been mindful of him,
>> mortal man that You have taken note of him?[1]

David's question is ultimately all encompassing. Is there a purpose to life, a reason to live in one way or another, a motivation to treat others with respect? Does God notice us? Does human life matter more than animal life? Is there an inherent difference between us and animals? Or are

---

1. Ps. 8:4–5 JPS (equals Ps. 8:3–4 NIV and NRSV).

we simply distinguishable from the rest of life on earth by being, in Plato's phrase, the only featherless bipeds?

Over the years and especially in the decades of the past century and a half, numerous voices have responded: "Man is an animal. Man is meat. Man is alone."

But David found a different answer:

> You have made him little less than divine,
> and adorned him with glory and majesty;
> You have made him master over Your handiwork,
> laying the world at his feet.[2]

David was not alone; he was a beloved son of his Creator. He and the greasy, smelly throng jostling each other around him as they pressed forward with their sheep and pigeons were the image of God.

What is the image of God? Theologians offer many different interpretations of this phrase, some of which we will examine later in this chapter. But do these interpretations, when plugged into an argument against abortion, for example, strengthen the argument? I fear that none of the most common understandings of God's image in humankind really does much to buttress an appeal to the inherent value of human beings. But, as Genesis 9:6 and James 3:9 indicate, God seems to think that our understanding of his image should make a difference. Worse, most of the explanations of God's image do not fit well with either the theology or the anthropology of the Bible.

In this book I will attempt to set forth an understanding of God's image that is biblically consistent, that finds pertinence in God's image throughout Scripture and theology, and that lays a firm foundation for recognizing the sanctity of human life.

Theories of God's Image

This book is not a review of all of the historical understandings of God's image, nor is it primarily a critique of them. Rather it is an explanation of a particular understanding of what is meant by God's image. A quick glance at some other interpretations, however, may help to paint the background on the stage as an aid to understanding the exegesis in the next few chapters. Therefore let us begin by looking briefly at the most common historic conceptions of the image of God. For our purposes we will be

---

2. Ps. 8:6–7 JPS (Ps. 8:5–6 NIV and NRSV).

Five Questions

generalizing to a very great extent, trying to see the broad pictures and not getting mired down in the minutia of intramural skirmishes.

We will have little need to consider or refute most of the ideas that have been suggested for understanding God's image. It should come as no surprise that over the past few thousand years quite a variety of understandings have emerged ostensibly answering to this concept. But if they currently have little hold, if they are not relevant to the discussion within the context of the main branches of post-Reformation theology, then we will have little to say about them. Indeed, to attempt to treat every contender for interpretive supremacy even of this one phrase would be a lifetime's work, for there are all too many theories crowding the stage.

Among the most constant and enduring contenders is the ancient Jewish understanding that humankind was made by angels, at God's prompting, and that therefore we are in the image of the angels who are in God's image.

> When the Holy One, blessed be He, wished to create man, He [first] created a company of ministering angels and said to them: Is it your desire that we make a man in our image?[3]

> GOD SAID, to His angels, "LET US MAKE MAN": So one also finds [God consulting his angels] in the story of Micaiah, son of Imlah, in Kings (I, 22.19–22) and in Isaiah (6.8), "Whom shall I send? Who will go for us?" and in Job (e.g. 1.6–12).[4]

A quick search on the Internet will show that this idea has found a home in many Protestant theologies. But the proposition hardly needs an answer, for the idea that the angels created us, or that we are made in their image, is so foreign to the biblical creation story that it constitutes a new story altogether rather than an explanation of the old story.

---

3. I. Epstein, ed., *The Babylonian Talmud: Seder Nezikin*, vol. 3, *Sanhedrin*, trans. Jacob Shachter and H. Freedman (London: Soncino Press, 1935), p. 242.

4. Martin I. Lockshin, *Rabbi Samuel Ben Meir's Commentary on "Genesis": An Annotated Translation* (Lewiston, N.Y.: Edwin Mellen, 1989), p. 51. A footnote to this passage mentions that "the plural forms that appear in God's speech in this verse naturally troubled the Jewish exegetes, particularly because this verse is, as David Berger put it, 'a *locus classicus* of trinitarian exegeses.' Rashbam follows the standard Jewish exegetical tradition by explaining that God was speaking to angels."

Attribute Theory of God's Image

An adaptation of this doctrine, that angels are God's image to a greater degree than are humans, was later taught by such a Christian luminary as St. Thomas Aquinas, who stated:

> We may speak of God's image in two ways.
>
> First, we may consider in it that in which the image chiefly consists, that is, the intellectual nature. Thus the image of God is more perfect in the angels than in man, because their intellectual nature is more perfect, as is clear from what has been said (58, 3; 79, 8).
>
> Secondly, we may consider the image of God in man as regards its accidental qualities, so far as to observe in man a certain imitation of God, consisting in the fact that man proceeds from man, as God from God; and also in the fact that the whole human soul is in the whole body, and again, in every part, as God is in regard to the whole world. In these and the like things the image of God is more perfect in man than it is in the angels. But these do not of themselves belong to the nature of the Divine image in man, unless we presuppose the first likeness, which is in the intellectual nature; otherwise even brute animals would be to God's image. Therefore, as in their intellectual nature, the angels are more to the image of God than man is, we must grant that, absolutely speaking, the angels are more to the image of God than man is, but that in some respects man is more like to God.[5]

Aquinas's statement of the doctrine was in some ways a simplification of St. Augustine's doctrine of the image being manifest in our trichotomy of being: body, mind, and soul. Having two such men in its pedigree, one can understand why the attribute theory held on despite its lack of credible exegetical support. Interestingly, the idea that the angels took part in the creation has been added back in by many who claim to follow Aquinas, although Aquinas himself rejected such a concept:

> We must not imagine that when God said "Let us make man," He spoke to the angels, as some were perverse enough to think. But by these words is signified the plurality of the Divine Person, Whose image is more clearly expressed in man.[6]

---

5. Thomas Aquinas, *Summa Theologica*, trans. Fathers of the English Dominican Province (London: Burns Oates & Washbourne, 1922), first part, quest. 93, art. 3, pp. 286–88.

6. Ibid., quest. 91, art. 4, pp. 271–73.

Five Questions

Official Roman Catholic teaching has largely followed Aquinas regarding God's image, as it has followed most of his teachings. Roman Catholic emphasis, however, usually rests on his exposition regarding wherein that image resides as regards humanity rather than in speculations about God's image in angels. "By virtue of his soul and his spiritual powers of intellect and will, man is endowed with freedom, an 'outstanding manifestation of the divine image.'" "The human person participates in the light and power of the divine Spirit. By his reason, he is capable of understanding the order of things established by the Creator. By free will, he is capable of directing himself toward his true good. He finds his perfection 'in seeking and loving what is true and good.'" "By his reason, man recognizes the voice of God."[7] Thus, official Roman Catholic teaching on this matter of God's image focuses on those universal powers and abilities of humans that enable us to live life in pursuit of godliness, in imitation of Christ. These qualities excel at defining that in humanity which could not and did not change after the Fall, or at least did not disappear. Catholicism thus succeeds in seeing a consistency to the image as it is exhibited at creation and in modern humankind.

Likewise, Eastern Orthodox theology is jealous to admit of no diminishing of the image in which Adam was created. Much as Catholicism does, Orthodox theology posits God's image exclusively in the ontological and permanent nature of humanity, that which makes humans human. As such, God's image is "the basic essence, the permanent and indestructible divine ground of his existence."[8] This "basic essence" is further delineated in terms of personality, reason, and freedom. We hear echoes of Augustine and Aquinas, and a clear parallel to the Roman Catholic Catechism.

Such interpretations of God's image, with their intent interest in finding God's image unchanged, tend toward a semi-Pelagian elevation of human spiritual ability and only a partial reliance on grace. Thus, to Eastern Orthodox theology, the image of God renders each human "capable, despite the darkening of his understanding, of seeking the truth and partially finding it."[9]

7. *Catechism of the Catholic Church*, Doctrines 1705, 1704, 1706, www.vatican.va/archive/ccc_css/archive/catechism/p3s1c1a1.htm.

8. Sergey Nikolayevich Bulgakov, "Die Christliche Anthropologie," *Kirche, Staat und Mensch. Russisch-orthodoxe Studiën* (Geneva: Forschungsabteilung des Oekumenischen rates für praktisches christentum, 1937), p. 223; quoted in G. C. Berkouwer, *Man: The Image of God*, trans. Dirk W. Jellema (Grand Rapids: Eerdmans, 1962), p. 49.

9. Serge Verkhowsky, "Die Lehre von Menschen im Lichte der orthodoxen Theologie," *Evangelische Theologie*, 11 (1951–52): 323; quoted in Berkouwer, *Man: The Image of God*, p. 50.

Therefore it is no surprise to find similar exclusively ontological interpretations of God's image among the most Arminian and semi-Pelagian of Protestant theologians. Among them, Charles Finney emphasized:

> Every sinner knows that sin is a willful abuse of his own powers as a moral agent—of those noblest powers of his being in view of which he is especially said to be made in the image of God. Made like God with these exalted attributes, capable of determining his own voluntary activities intelligently if he will; in accordance with his reason and his conscience if he will; he yet in every act of sin abuses and degrades these powers, tramples down in the very dust the image of God enstamped on his being, and with the capacities of becoming an angel, makes himself a fool.[10]
>
> The image of God in which man was created, could not possibly have related to his moral character, for moral character is not a subject of creation.[11]

For ease of language, and because it is held in greater or lesser degree by theologians with a wide variety of theological loyalties, let us call this group of proposals "attribute theory." Attribute theory thus finds God's image in those attributes, however they may be delineated by any particular theologian or anthropologist, which are considered to be universal to the human condition and were not lost at the Fall. Therefore, those who fit neatly into this camp will agree that human sin has not destroyed God's image, although they may argue about the exact dimensions of that image.

Is such a demarcation of God's image not radically flawed in that it portrays a stick figure God? It makes God too small, too flat, and too easily imaged. Can we really imagine that God's idea of his own image is mud people who exhibit "faculties and principles of nature," regardless of how those faculties and principles are delineated? Are we so much vaster than Almighty God that we can portray his image adequately in one facet of our lives (for are not each of these attributes but mere facets of our larger selves?), a facet in which we do not participate for the first part of our lives and in which many people never do? Attribute theory does not see humanity portraying God's entire image, and even worse, it sees God's image being portrayed by mere fragments of our selves. If one set out to paint a

---

10. Charles Finney, "Where Sin Occurs, God Can Not Wisely Prevent," *The Oberlin Evangelist* (August 2, 1854), www.gospeltruth.net/1854OE/540802_where_sin_occurs.

11. Ibid., "Affections and Emotions of God," *The Oberlin Evangelist* 1, no. 22 (October 9, 1839), p. 168.

self-portrait, would one be satisfied to portray only the nail on one's pinky toe? And yet does not the theory described above see God doing just that in making an image of himself that can be portrayed in just one small aspect of our experience of being human?

It strikes me as interesting that this theory, the most enduring understanding of God's image within the years since Jesus ascended, is the one that is most clearly denied in Scripture:

> To whom, then, will you compare God?
>   What image will you compare him to?
> "To whom will you compare me?
>   Or who is my equal?" says the Holy One.
> "For my thoughts are not your thoughts,
>   neither are your ways my ways," declares the LORD.
> "As the heavens are higher than the earth,
>   so are my ways higher than your ways
>   and my thoughts than your thoughts."[12]

John Wesley, while agreeing with most of what we have quoted from Finney and using similar words regarding humankind's natural powers, intelligence, and "government of himself by the freedom of his will," demanded more of God's image. In addition to humankind's natural powers, he saw in the concept of God's image an "habitual conformity of all his natural powers to the whole will of God."

> Thus holy, thus happy, were our first parents, in having the image of God upon them. But how art thou fallen, O son of the morning? How is this image of God upon man defaced![13]

For him, mere human traits were too little to answer to so great a concept as the image of God. Here John Wesley, like Arminius, who likewise saw a duality of "natural" (ontological and inalienable) and "accidental" (resulting from actions) traits, provides a bridge to the Lutheran and Reformed theologies of God's image, for they too insist on an aspect of God's image that has been lost, and may be regained only in Jesus.[14]

---

12. Isa. 40:18, 25; 55:8–9 NIV.

13. *John Wesley's Notes*, comment on Gen. 1:26, www.ccel.org/w/wesley/notes/.

14. The distinction between the natural and the accidental aspects of God's image is laid out especially in *The Works of James Arminius*, "Disputation XXVI, On the Creation of Man After the Image of God," www.ccel.org/arminius/works2.html. Here we can see that Arminius was not entirely as "Arminian" as some who bear his name.

Purity Theory of God's Image

Martin Luther, for instance, could see no vestige of God's image either in himself or in his contemporaries.

> Since the loss of this image through sin we cannot understand it to any extent. Memory, will, and mind we have indeed; but they are most depraved and most seriously weakened, yes, to put it more clearly, they are utterly leprous and unclean. If these powers are the image of God, it will also follow that Satan was created according to the image of God, since he surely has these natural endowments, such as memory and a very superior intellect and a most determined will, to a far higher degree than we have them. Therefore when we speak about that image, we are speaking about something unknown. Not only have we no experience of it, but we continually experience the opposite; and so we hear nothing but bare words.[15]

What makes God's image so foreign according to Martin Luther? It is the Fall, Adam's plummet into sin, in which we fell with him. Luther saw that there is no Scriptural warrant for all of the philosophical speculation that goes into formulating the analogy-of-being that ties us to God in the attribute theory. He recognized how foreign such abstracting of one portion of a person from another portion is to Scripture. Rather, the Bible sees whole humans in relation to each other and in relation to God. And at the Fall these relations, especially the relation to God, were severed. Adam, being created in righteousness and devoted service to God, had lived in conformity to God's will. Adam had loved as God loves, dreamed as God dreams, and worked as God works. In this conformity Adam had been a mirror of God, a likeness of God, the image of God.

But at the Fall, according to Luther, all of that changed. Adam and all of his posterity no longer would exhibit any conformity to God; hence they could in no way be called an image of God. This is after all the standard by which the Bible tends to judge people: do they judge as God judges? Do they love what God loves? Do they have a heart after his heart, in conformity to his?

Thus, Martin Luther has taken sin seriously; he has seen the devastating effects of sin on the individual human. We are mere shells compared to the blessed creatures that God placed in the garden. The attribute theorists

---

15. *Luther's Works*, vol. 1, *Lectures on Genesis, Chapters 1–5*, ed. Jaroslav Pelikan and trans. George V. Schick (Saint Louis: Concordia Publishing House, 1958), pp. 63–64.

would do well to listen to Luther on this; we are no longer what we were. We have lost much more than our home.

We can call this idea the "purity theory" of God's image, for it sees God's image exclusively in the original purity in which we were created and in that regained purity that is available in Christ. Hence, the goal of Jesus on the earth, on the cross, and on the throne is to bring us back into that relationship with him in which we once walked. This creates a theology of Paradise lost and regained, in which we, being strangers in this land east of Eden, are seeking to return to our first home.

But does the Bible primarily represent God as working to bring us back to Eden? Is our goal to walk again by the river Euphrates and eat of the fruit of God's garden? Does the biblical map of history look like a loop, or like a line? Is biblical eschatology always looking back to the garden as its goal? Is it not rather forward looking? Though our story began in a garden, it is fulfilled in a city. The great hope of Christians is not once again to have God walk with us in the cool of the day, but rather to be united to Jesus night and day. If we wish to walk again naked in the garden, we will first have to cast off the robes in which God has promised to clothe us. We have a far greater hope than simply to return to Eden.

Also, while the Bible is vehement that we are cut off from God through our sin, there is no hint in Scripture that this excludes us from God's image. Rather, the Bible continues to call humankind God's image long after the Fall, and no distinction is made that would exclude sinners and include only saints within the compass of the term.

A Dualistic Approach

G. C. Berkouwer, following Herman Bavinck and other Reformed theologians, distinguishes between a "wider" and a "narrower" sense of God's image. The wider is very much in line with what we have termed attribute theory, those aspects that distinguish humanity from other creatures. This wider sense was deemed necessary to assure that "man, despite his fall into sin, was not bestialized or demonized, but remained man."[16] In this respect Abraham Kuyper, Jr., says that the essence of what it means to be human is to be "a reasonable and spiritual being, or, a being with an individual ego which has two faculties, namely, to know and to will."[17] This, the broader aspect of God's image as postulated by many Reformed theologians, is

---

16. Berkouwer, *Man: The Image of God*, p. 38.

17. Abraham Kuyper, Jr., *Het Beeld Gods* (1929), p. 64; quoted in Berkouwer, *Man: The Image of God*, p. 39.

"an indestructible element in man's constitution [comprising] reason, conscience, freedom, etc."[18]

In contrast to this universal sense, what these Reformed theologians have termed the "narrower sense" of God's image stresses that humanity no longer exists in the same state in which it was formed; it no longer enjoys communion with God, holiness, or perfect peace in desiring just as God desires. The *Canons of Dort* expound this narrow sense of God's image:

> Man, from the beginning was created in the image of God, adorned in his mind, with the true and saving knowledge of his Creator and of spiritual things, with righteousness in his will and heart, and purity in all his affections, and thus was altogether holy; but . . . revolting from God, he bereaved himself of these inestimable gifts.[19]

As the *Heidelberg Catechism* explains this narrower aspect of God's image, "God created man good and in his image, that is, in true righteousness and holiness."[20]

Both the wider and the narrower aspects of God's image are defined by Jonathan Edwards, although he like John Calvin does not use the terminology of "wider" and "narrower."

> And herein does very much consist that image of God wherein He made man (which we read of, Gen. i. 26, 27, and chap. ix. 6), by which God distinguished man from the beasts, *viz.* in those faculties and principles of nature, whereby he is capable of moral agency. Herein very much consists the natural image of God; as his spiritual and moral image, wherein man was made at first, consisted in that moral excellency that he was endowed with.[21]

By "capable of moral agency," Edwards meant that humans exhibit a will, rational thought, planning, and so on. In other words, he found that we largely resemble God in our intellectual powers. There is the wider image, the same unchangeable attributes that we saw above when considering proposals of Catholicism and Arminianism. But Edwards also saw the im-

---

18. James Orr, *God's Image in Man* (1948), p. 59; quoted in Berkouwer, *Man: The Image of God*, p. 40.

19. *The Articles of the Synod of Dort*, ed. and trans. Thomas Scott (Utica, N.Y.: William Williams, 1831), p. 105.

20. *Heidelberg Catechism*, "Answer to Question 6," in *Reformed Confessions of the 16th Century*, ed. Arthur C. Cochrane (Philadelphia: Westminster Press, [1966]), p. 306.

21. Jonathan Edwards, *The Freedom of the Will* (Morgan, Pa.: Soli Deo Gloria Publications, 1996), pp. 35–36.

age of God in our original purity that we lost at the Fall. God's image was to be seen in the moral perfection that Adam and Eve possessed at their creation. Here is the narrower image.

This narrow sense of God's image was not inalienable; it was mutable and has been lost, according to many Reformed theologians. Thus John Calvin explains that "God's image is the perfect excellence of human nature which shone in Adam before his defection, but was subsequently so vitiated and almost blotted out that nothing remains after the ruin except what is confused, mutilated, and disease-ridden."[22]

But many Reformed theologians were profoundly uncomfortable with the dualism that was thus set up between the two images. This was, after all, a theory that proposed two images to answer to the same name. And John Calvin had even insisted that our bodies were physically part of God's image, making three separate images, all answering to the same name that is always given in the singular in Scripture.

But the idea of even two images produces an unsettling dualism. Among the many Reformed theologians who were profoundly disturbed by this dualism, Herman Bavinck seems to have made the most headway toward alleviating it. He insisted that the two concepts must not be held individually, as separate concepts, but must be melded and seen as organically related. Unfortunately, he was not able to explain what he meant by "organically related" or how the two aspects were to be melded.

They are simply too different. That is why two senses of the term were used, because theologians saw disparate concepts to which they thought that they must affix the term *imago Dei*. But this radical difference makes them poor candidates to be reunited as a single organic concept.

In the Reformed tradition it became customary to hold two radically different ideas of what God's image was and, in fact, to hold them in tandem. This dualism was a concession to biblical evidence that was thought to point in both directions. Genesis 9:6 and James 3:9 each confirm that God did not cease to call us his image after the Fall, but Reformed theologians could find no likeness to God in our ethical and spiritual lives. Therefore they sought to find place for both positions.

As mentioned above, the first of these ideas, the wider aspect of God's image, corresponds closely with what we have called the attribute theory of God's image. For our purposes of generalizing we may leave it there.

The second concept, the narrower aspect of God's image, being the one that was lost at the Fall and is regained only in Christ, is nearly

---

22. John Calvin, *Institutes of the Christian Religion*, ed. John T. McNeill and trans. Ford Lewis Battles (Philadelphia: Westminster Press, 1960), pp. 188–90.

equivalent to the Lutheran concept that we have called the purity theory of God's image. Therefore, we can speak of the historic Reformed doctrine of God's image as being an attempt to hold both the attribute theory and the purity theory in tandem, more or less equivalently, and unfortunately dualistically. By incorporating (albeit with subtle modifications) both the attribute and the purity models of God's image, this Reformed doctrine falls prey to nearly all of the criticisms made of them, but especially to the charge of dualism.

Physical Theory of God's Image

We have mentioned that John Calvin insisted not only that the inalienable traits of humanness and the lost blessings of holiness were contained in the phrase "image of God," but he also included the physical makeup of the human body. "Although the primary seat of the divine image was in the mind and heart, or in the soul and its powers, yet there was no part of man, not even the body itself, in which some sparks did not glow."[23] Calvin is here postulating that in some way our bodies analogically point to our Creator. He is not insinuating, although it has been taught from the very earliest times and still is taught by many others, that our bodies resemble God's body. Calvin understood God to be spirit and to have no body; hence any image of God in our bodies would be by analogy.

This "physical likeness" theory has been the source of much interesting speculation over the years. Some have proposed that our bodies point us toward God in that while all other mammals walk about on four legs with their heads looking down, we walk upright (do you hear the analogy, an upright man?) with our eyes to heaven. Therefore we are meant for heavenly things while the animals are meant for earthly.

And it has gotten worse. Consider a couple of lines from a sermon.

> Men, do you remember the first time you saw a beautiful woman without any clothes on? Now that's breathtaking! There's no need to be embarrassed by how powerful such an image is. It is, after all, an image of God.[24]

But there is no need to look to the most crass expressions of this physical likeness theory. It suffers from deficiencies similar to those of the

---

23. Calvin, *Institutes of the Christian Religion*, p. 188.

24. Robert M. Bowman, "My God, How Great Thou Art, Sermon for the Transfiguration," delivered at United Catholic Church, Melbourne, Fla., March 7–8, 1998, www.rmbowman.com/catholic/s980307h.htm.

attribute theory. It calls for endless speculation, speculation in which the Bible will be of little help unless help is wrung from it against its will. For instance, we could find an analogy from our bodies to God's strength and power which he refers to often enough as his "arm." "Is the LORD's arm too short?"[25] Here we might see an analogy to God in that we have arms in which we exhibit our strength and power. Or how about our nostrils? "Such people are smoke in my nostrils."[26] That must be it! I resemble God because smoke burns my nostrils and annoys me just as wicked people annoy God. But God also seems to have feathers and wings; he even compares himself to a hen.[27] Are the clucking Leghorn hens strutting around in the yard scratching for seeds and bugs also God's image in that they exhibit feathers and wings? Can we not find an analogy (if analogy is all that is needed to be God's image) for God in almost anything if we use a little imagination? How useful would it be for God to tell us that we can find analogies to himself in our bodies?

And, as with the attribute theory above, we seem to see a one-dimensional God if he will be displayed adequately in our bodies. Even if we combine the attribute theory, which focuses on our psychological makeup and our capacities, with the physical likeness theory, we still are left with a very partial God who is said to be displayed on a tiny fraction of ourselves. But God's proposal, "Let us make humankind in our image," seems to indicate that it will involve all of us and all of him, or all of them.

Multiple Understandings

Many other understandings have been proposed over the years, and many theologians will affirm portions of a number of them. In all of the above we have endeavored to give just the simplest of outlines, and many theologians will differ significantly from the position into which they might seem to be expected to fit. Nevertheless, for the purpose of providing a background for the following chapters, it is sufficient.

After contemplating a much longer list of explanations for the meaning of God's image, Karl Barth pointedly remarks,

25. Num. 11:23 NIV.

26. Isa. 65:5 NIV.

27. References ascribing physical characteristics to God are too numerous to make a comprehensive list. Regarding wings, feathers, and hens, begin with Ps. 91:4; Exod. 19:4; Ruth 2:12; Ps. 17:8, 61:4; Matt. 23:37; and Luke 13:34. A delightful guide for the interpretation of such physical descriptions of God can be found in Benjamin Keach, *Tropologia, A Key to Open Scripture Metaphors* (London: Printed by J. R. and J. D. for E. Prosser, 1682).

We might easily discuss which of these and the many other similar explanations is the finest or deepest or most serious. What we cannot discuss is which of them is the true explanation of Gen. 1:26f. For it is obvious that their authors merely found the conception in the text and then proceeded to pure invention in accordance with the requirements of contemporary anthropology, so that it is only by the standard of contemporary anthropology, and not according to the measure of its own anthropology and on exegetical grounds, that we can decide for or against them.[28]

There is, I will suggest below, another understanding in which God's image is more fundamental to human nature than the commonly held views suggest, and in which God's image is seen to be more pervasive throughout the whole of human personhood and over all of history, past, present, and future.

Our Role as God's Image

Before we begin the long task of exegeting the words of Genesis 1:26, it would perhaps be well to take a quick glance at the end of it all, the doctrine toward which we will be working. Here, in a nutshell, is the doctrine of God's image that will be defended in the following chapters.

God is jealous for the blood (life) of humans not because we *carry* his image, but because we *are* his image. Scripture does not say that God implanted his image inside of us as an addition to us, but that we are his image. This is the only basis that I know of for affirming human dignity and worth. Human dignity comes not from any traits inside of ourselves, but from a role imposed upon us by our Creator at the time of our creation. As long as we exist we will be in this role. All of the personality characteristics which are so often debated with respect to the image of God are merely that: characteristics. God did not make mankind with his image as one, or some, or all of our characteristics. God made humans expressly to *be* his image.

This is the one central and essential point that sets up the difference between us and the animals: they were not created to be the image of God; we were. This was Adam's role in the newly created universe, and this is the role into which every one of Adam's descendents is born. We are the image and likeness, the picture, to which all of creation looks to see the invisible God. The birds and fish, the stars and angels are to look to us to see what

---

28. Karl Barth, *Church Dogmatics* (Edinburgh: T. & T. Clark, 1958), 3,1:193.

their Creator is like. Even more fundamentally, God is to be able to see his own glory reflected in us.

But we do not look like God in our actions, thoughts, or motives. We do not display his image well. At first glance we do not appear to be much like our Creator. Does this mean that we are no longer in the image of God? Has God's image failed, or disappeared? Not at all, for this again assumes that this image is either an attribute or an achievement, something added to us aside from our essential person. It is not. One could view it as a commandment. We are commanded to exhibit God's image, and although we fall short, the commandment of God will never fall.

Five Pertinent Questions

Gordon J. Wenham has noted that nearly all analyses of Genesis 1:26 have focused on three questions:[29]

1. Why does God speak in the plural (us/our)? Why did he not say, "Let me make man in my image?"
2. What is the force of the prepositions בְּ (*b-*, in) and כְּ (*k-*, according to) in this passage?
3. What is meant by צֶלֶם (*tselem*, image) and דְּמוּת (*demuth*, likeness)? Is there any difference between the terms here?

We will add two more questions that should be asked but too rarely are:

4. What is meant by the word אָדָם (*adam*, man)?
5. Why does God propose to "make" us rather than to "create" or "form" us?

Let us turn to these questions in the order they appear in Genesis 1:26, both in the English and the Hebrew texts. Therefore, we will address questions 1, 5, 4, 2, and 3, in that order.

---

29. Gordon J. Wenham, *Genesis*, vol. 1, *One Through Fifteen* (Waco, Texas: Word Books, 1987), p. 27.

2

Let Us Make

PRIOR TO the creation of humanity, when God filled the world with life, he simply called forth the creatures and all was done according to his word. He said repeatedly, "Let there be" and "Let the waters bring forth" and "Let the earth bring forth," and with each command the thing called forth appeared. The word "let" does not really appear in the original as a separate word, but is commonly added in translation to make clear that God was calling forth rather than speaking to the creation. When God said, "Let the waters bring forth," he was not speaking to the waters themselves as if he were commanding them, "Waters, you must bring forth." Rather, with his word the deed was accomplished.[1]

    The creation story itself never makes clear to whom God was speaking. That God's Spirit was involved in creation can be seen from the reference to his "hovering over the waters."[2] The Psalmist also declares, "When you send forth your spirit, they are created; and you renew the face of the ground."[3] However, it is difficult to imagine any monotheist reading these passages and understanding them to refer to a separate person who is also God unless that reader were a prophet or were enlightened by the New Testament. Not until the New Testament do we see clearly that the Holy Spirit is a separate individual and find a name for the Father's other partner in this work. "In these last days he has spoken to us by a Son, whom he appointed heir of all things, through whom he also created the worlds."[4] "There is one God, the Father, from whom are all things and for whom we exist, and one Lord, Jesus Christ, through whom are all things and through whom we exist."[5] The idea that God created all things *through*

---

    1. The discussion of Hebrew grammar in this chapter is indebted to works by Gordon J. Wenham, Lee Martin, and Gerhard Kittel, and to the notes of the New English Translation (NET) Bible.

    2. Gen. 1:2 NIV.

    3. Ps. 104:30 NRSV.

    4. Heb. 1:2 NRSV.

    5. 1 Cor. 8:6 NRSV.

Jesus indicates that God the Father was speaking in the Genesis creation record to his Son through whom he made the world. The passages quoted above from the Psalms and from Genesis indicate that he also was likely addressing his Spirit. Thus, a reading informed by the New Testament allows that the Father could have been addressing both his Son and his Spirit throughout the account of the creation. We will consider this question more carefully in a few pages.

Let

The grammatical construction of the "let-there-be" commands of Genesis chapter 1 is known as the jussive voice; that is, it is a modified imperative in the third person, which expresses will. It has the force of saying, "It is my will that the earth produce. . . ." And we see that God's will is able to accomplish its fulfillment immediately. He is calling the creation forth, but he is not speaking directly to it as if he had said, "Earth, produce . . . ," or "Fish, swarm the seas."

In contrast to these, in 1:26 when God says, "Let us make," he is speaking not in the jussive but in the cohortative voice. This cohortative voice is a modified first person (as opposed to the third person of the jussive voice) imperative "expressing desire, will, request, wish, self-encouragement, intention of the speaker for himself."[6] John Skinner contrasts God's words in this final creation to his words in the previous creations in that "instead of the simple jussive we have the cohortative of either self-deliberation or consultation with other divine beings,"[7] but he then rejects the possibility that it could be both of these at once. Being in the plural here, the cohortative is a call for unanimity of intentions and actions.

As also in the jussive, the force of God's will here is not directly toward the creatures whom he is calling forth, but toward the unanimity

---

6. Lee Martin, *A Dictionary of Special and Technical Terms for Hebrew and Greek Studies*, http//earth.vol.com/~lmartin/HBGKDICT.HTM.

7. John Skinner, *A Critical and Exegetical Commentary on Genesis* (New York: Charles Scribner's Sons, 1925), p. 30. Insisting that the plural "Let *us*" cannot be a reference to the Trinity because "that doctrine is entirely unknown to the OT," he then proposes that God was consulting and requesting help from the host of heaven, the angels. Even while he argues for that interpretation, he admits that "the very existence of angels is nowhere alluded to by" the author of this creation passage, and that his interpretation "ascribes to angels some share in the creation of man, which is contrary to scriptural doctrine," pp. 30-31. Nevertheless, he is willing to reject the Trinitarian option that is in keeping with both New Testament and Old Testament witness. Such an argument seems to be like a man's desperately grabbing hold of a wave to pull himself out of a boat into the safety of the sea.

of purpose and endeavor with which this act of creation is to be accomplished. It is that unanimity which he is here calling forth. It would not be an exaggeration to translate the verb in 1:26 as, "It is my fixed purpose that we unite to create. . . ." Compare the plea in the letter to the Hebrews, "Let us run with perseverance the race that is set before us."[8] There is no idea here of many individual believers racing against one another. We are not each being called (in this particular passage) to prepare for individual races that God has set before each one of us, as if this were a parallel to Jesus' call for each to pick up the individual cross that is set before her or him. The author is calling for all to run together, as one body, the race (singular) that is set before the church as a whole. Similarly, see the account of the building of the tower at Babel where the people said, "Let us make bricks" and "Let us build ourselves a city." No expositor would suggest that the people were proposing that each individual make his or her own individual city. In these we can see clearly how the cohortative voice carries the idea, "Let us unite for a single purpose."

Us

At this point we would do well to consider more deeply the question of to whom God was speaking when he called for unanimity of mind and endeavor in creating. Who is "us"? Was God, in fact, addressing the hosts of heaven? Is this construction a reference to the Trinity? Or could God be using a plural of majesty? Both the importance of the answer to this question and the variety of answers that have been given to it prompt us to look again at the question—to whom could God be speaking?—and to examine more closely several popular answers to it.

If God had been calling on the angels, as is often suggested, to participate in the creation of humanity, then the next plural, "our image," would indicate that we were being created in the image of the angels just as much as in God's own image. Not only would this interpretation be difficult to fit in with the rest of the biblical account of creation, but also in the very next verse we are told that "God created man in his own image."[9] We are not made in the image of God *and* his angels. We are also met with the difficulty that nowhere in the rest of Scripture are the angels said to be part of the process of creation.

The idea that God could be using a plural of majesty has been put forward by some commentators. However, we are faced with the problem

8. Heb. 12:1 NRSV.
9. Gen. 1:27 NIV.

that God does not elsewhere refer to himself with such a plural. The word "Elohim," although plural, always has a singular verb associated with it when it refers to Jehovah. It is "plural in form but singular in meaning."[10] Whether God is deliberating ("I will make him a helper"[11]) or considering his own majesty ("I the LORD your God am a jealous God"[12]), he always uses the singular of himself. If God had used the plural of majesty to refer to himself at the creation, would he not have continued to do so? And linguistically it has been shown that "the plural of majesty is not used with verbs."[13] That is, it is not left as an inference to be made by the hearer or reader. The plural of majesty must always be explicit, as a plural noun or pronoun. In Genesis 1:26 the word "us" is not a separate word in the Hebrew, but is included in the verb. In order to function as a plural of majesty, plurality would need to be expressed by an actual noun or pronoun and not just left as an implied pronoun. This distinction is less clear to us in English, for nearly all of our pronouns are expressed, but the distinction is obvious in Hebrew. Because of this fact, few scholars still support the plural of majesty interpretation.

Also, the cohortative voice of the plural verb would tend to render difficult a singular understanding of the plural antecedent. In other words, the plural of majesty (in effect a singular) would not make sense of God's call for unanimity in the endeavor. Such a meaning on God's part would have required a singular cohortative voice (singular in the verb even if a plural of majesty were used for the noun/pronoun) rather than a plural cohortative. Even if it were here to be understood as a singular cohortative (difficult though that would be), we then would have the problem of understanding why God was trying to psyche himself up to some great feat. The singular cohortative works for humans, for we at times need to prepare ourselves before we undertake a work. Consider Prince Hamlet's words as he is plotting to murder his uncle:

> When he is drunk asleep, or in his rage,
> Or in th' incestuous pleasure of his bed,
> At game a-swearing, or about some act
> That has no relish of salvation in't—
> Then trip him, that his heels may kick at heaven,

---

10. Gordon J. Wenham, *Word Biblical Commentary*, vol. 1, *Genesis 1–15* (Waco, Tex.: Word Books, 1987), p. 14.

11. Gen. 2:18 NRSV.

12. Exod. 20:5 NRSV.

13. Wenham, *Genesis*, p. 28.

> And that his soul may be as damned and black
> As hell, whereto it goes.[14]

He might have used the cohortative singular had he been speaking in Hebrew. But God is not Hamlet, trying to steel his nerve to murder. Nor is he a little boy standing on the end of a diving board, saying, "Okay, here goes. Three, two, one. . . . No, wait; one, two, three. . . . Okay, here goes . . . ." No, this is a plural verb, and it functions as a plural; there is just no legitimate way to make a singular out of it. So let us consider the other common option for the meaning of God's "let us."

The understanding that the plural is God the Father speaking to the other members of the Trinity has fallen on disfavor in the past century and a half of textual criticism and scholarship. Long held as the standard orthodox view, "it is now universally admitted that this was not what the plural meant to the original author."[15] This "universal" change has taken place largely as a result of an evolutionary understanding of the text of Genesis as being not the work of Moses writing the Word of God, but as a compilation of ancient stories, legends, and myths that were compiled and fitted together by an editor. François Lenormant expressed in 1882 what has since come to be the most common assumption among Old Testament scholars: "It is not an account dictated by God himself. . . . It is a tradition . . . which all the great nations of Western Asia possessed in common, with some variations."[16] With such a conception of the roots of Genesis, scholars reasonably expect the editor to impose his own theology on the text, and Trinitarian "insights were certainly beyond the horizon of the editor of Genesis."[17]

But what if the recent scholars are wrong? What if Genesis really is the work of one man, Moses, who wrote the whole Torah (Law)? Jesus seems to have assumed as much when he referred to all of what we call the Old Testament as "the law of Moses, the prophets, and the psalms."[18]

---

14. William Shakespeare, *Hamlet* (New York: Washington Square Press, 1992), act 3, scene 3.

15. Wenham, *Genesis*, p. 27.

16. François Lenormant, *The Beginnings of History According to the Bible and the Traditions of the Oriental Peoples, From the Creation to the Deluge* (New York: Charles Scribner's Son, 1882), p. xv; I am indebted to Gunnlaugur A. Jónsson, *The Image of God: Genesis 1:26–28 in a Century of Research* (Stockholm: Almqvist & Wiksell International, 1988), p. 22, for this reference.

17. Wenham, *Genesis*, p. 28.

18. Luke 24:44 NRSV.

Let Us Make

When Jesus referred to the "law of Moses," how many books did he have in mind?

The word "Torah," when used not as a reference to specific laws but as an overall term for a book or written law, could be used for any of three related bodies of written law. First is the law proper, or the Decalogue plus the other Sinai laws. While Torah could be used of the Decalogue by itself, it more generally referred to the whole body of the Sinai law together. Hence, although the morning recitation of the Decalogue at the Second Temple had been a popular practice for years, it had to be abandoned in later years. As Rabbi Matna explained, "Truly one should recite the Ten Commandments daily; and why does one not recite them? Because one does not wish to give a foothold to the assertions of heretics, that they may not be able to say that these alone were given on Sinai."[19]

In fact, the Pentateuch was not really considered to be five books in the Hebrew Bible, but only one, as when Jesus referred to "the book of Moses."[20] One book of Moses, not five books, and that one book of Moses included all of Genesis. To be blunt, Jesus did not believe in Lenormant's editor hypothesis. If Jesus were able by the breath of his mouth to create the universe and us, if his word will cast sin and death into an eternal pit, why is his word invalid when he ascribed the Pentateuch to the pen of Moses? Jesus I know, and Moses I know, but who is Lenormant?

These days, if you were to go into a Jewish bookstore and request an Old Testament, the proprietor would direct you to a shelf of books entitled, *Tanakh*. That word is made up in just the same way that our word NASA is, by taking the first letters of words and using them to form a new word. This new word is then treated just as any other word, except that it takes many years to lose the capitalization of the letters. We do not say each letter, but rather we read the set of letters as a word, "NASA." Similarly, the Hebrew word "Tanakh" is formed from the initial letters of: *Torah* (Law or Pentateuch), *Nevi'im* (Prophets), and *Kethuvim* (Writings).[21] Notice the similarity between this modern term for the Hebrew Scriptures

---

19. Cited in H. Kleinecht and W. Gutbrod, "νομοσ," in *Theological Dictionary of the New Testament*, edited by Gerhard Kittel (Grand Rapids: Eerdmans, 1967), 4:1054.

20. Mark 12:26 NRSV.

21. For information on the word "Tanakh" and on the breakdown of the three main sections of the *Tanakh*, see the preface to the 1985 English edition of the *JPS Hebrew-English Tanakh* (Philadelphia: The Jewish Publication Society, 1999), or see the glossary of the Jewish Virtual Library (www.jewishvirtuallibrary.org).

and the one that Jesus used, "the Law of Moses, the Prophets and the Psalms."[22]

If we accept that Moses penned the Torah, then these problems of the "editor" will disappear. Moses did not need to understand fully all that God said in order to write it down faithfully. These words are not Moses' commentary, but his record of what God said.

Because the words "let us make" were said before there were any people to hear, the words recorded are either mythological (in the old and common sense of that word) or they were given to the author by divine revelation. This disjunctive choice applies to all that is recorded of the creation. If mythological (perhaps legendary or apocryphal would be more precise), then God and the whole Bible will be discredited for that which is called the Law (*Torah*) of Moses is also called the Law (*Torah*) of God.[23] Because the New Testament presupposes the Torah and Jesus' authority on earth rests on his having "authored" it, the New Testament's credibility will fall if the Torah does. If these words are not a direct quote from God, then it would be foolish for us to waste another second wondering what they mean.

If not mythological, then the words can be taken as God's spoken words, which do not need to be fully understood by Moses, by a hypothetical editor, or by me for them to be valid. God told Adam that he would die from eating the fruit of one tree. Before we can understand this statement, do we need to ask what Adam understood it to mean? No, we have greater knowledge than Adam did and we can see what he could not have. God said that the serpent would strike the heel of Eve's offspring and her offspring would strike his head. Did Moses, an editor, or Eve understand this prophecy fully? Does our perspective not bless us with greater understanding of what God meant? Must we limit our understanding to that of the original hearers?

Neither should we limit the possible meaning of God's words spoken before our creation to only those meanings which we think likely would have been in the mind of some hypothetical editor. We know that all three persons of the Trinity were involved in the creation. God's Spirit is active in Genesis 1:2 as well as in Psalm 104, and the Son is often referred to in Scripture as being creator.[24] Reference to the active participation of all three persons of the Trinity in creation seems to be the only understanding

---

22. Luke 24:44 NIV.
23. Neh. 10:29 NIV: "the Law of God given through Moses."
24. Heb. 1:2; John 1:3; Col. 1:16; etc.

that makes sense of the plural verb "let us," the plural "our" prefixed to a singular "image," the use of the cohortative voice, and the testimony of the whole of Scripture. Therefore, it is perfectly reasonable that we should see God's call for cooperation in the creation of humankind as a call to the Spirit and the Son.

The triune manner of working in the first (material) creation is mirrored in the triune working in the second (salvific) creation. In terms of the image of God, the two creations are united. In the first creation, God the Father called forth the creatures by name, and similarly in the second he calls out by name those whom he has given to his Son. The Son was the mediator of both creations; the world was made by and through him, and salvation came by and through him, always at his Father's command. The Spirit's work in the first creation is less clear, although Psalm 104:30 seems to suggest that God's continual upholding and perpetuating—that is, his providential renewing of creation—is accomplished by his Spirit. Renewing, perpetuating, and upholding are also part of the Spirit's role in the new creation. Such parallels add weight and clarity to the interpretation that God the Father was addressing his Son and his Spirit in all of the creation directives, be they "let-there-be" or "let-us-make."

In fine, God's image is a Trinitarian creation. As such, it is based on the solid decree of the Father; hence, it cannot be negated by us. It is covenantally inaugurated, with an oath and God the Son's own blood; hence it is eternal and cannot be negated by us. It is providentially upheld by the Spirit; hence it is eternally renewed and cannot be negated by us. These statements will be filled out by the end of this book. To say that Adam destroyed the image of God, or even damaged it, when he bit into a fruit is like saying that he became a bachelor again whenever he closed his eyes. Not being able to see his wife did not free him from his obligations to her. No more does our wickedness free us from God's image, so great is his loving kindness toward us.

3

Make, Create, and Form

WHAT, IF any, significance is there to God's use of the word "make" in his proposal "Let us make mankind"? How are the three main creation words, "create," "make," and "form," similar and how different? At various times they are grouped together, and the fact that they occur together as parallels makes clear that there is considerable similarity between them, but with any set of synonyms there must be differences also. When the three of them appear together, for instance when God says, "everyone who is called by my name, whom I created for my glory, whom I formed and made,"[1] it seems clear that God is using the words as synonyms. Yet at the same time he is not stuttering; he is not repeating precisely the same thing each time.

Let us first look individually at the words "to create," "to form," and "to make," before we consider them in relation to God's making Adam, and *adam*.[2] We will begin by considering the usual lexical questions: What action is performed? Who typically performs this action? After establishing answers to these questions, we will return to each verb to consider questions of nuance: What function does this sentence play in the context? What role within the sentence is played by each verb? What implications accompany the use of each verb?

בָּרָא (To Create), Part 1

בָּרָא (*bara'*, to create) is a word reserved exclusively for the works of God. In the Hebrew Bible God is said to have created the heavens and the earth; that is, he created the universe, all that we see. He created the sea

---

1. Isa. 43:7 NIV; see also Deut. 32:6 and Isa. 45:18.

2. The Hebrew word אָדָם is transliterated into English as *adam*. While we will use the word *adam* throughout, we will look at the term in more depth in chapter 4 when we consider the meaning of "man" in God's phrase "Let us make man. . . ." Briefly, "Adam" represents the name of an individual, our first parent. In italics and without the capital the transliterated Hebrew word "*adam*" represents humanity considered simultaneously as individuals and as a group.

monsters, humankind, the wind and the stars. He created Israel, both the individual and the nation. He created his people and called them by his own name. At one point or another we see that God created all that is, not only on earth, but also above and below the earth. He created angels and the armies of heaven; he created the cherub Satan and his minions.[3]

He also creates events, not only creatures. In fact, God declares:

> I form the light and create darkness,
> I bring prosperity and create disaster.[4]

He creates darkness and disaster; in the King James Version this last phrase is rendered as "I make peace, and create evil," which has caused no end of questions from young Christians. But we see from the juxtaposition that is set up between the words "peace" (*shalom*) and "evil" (*ra'*) that it is the antithesis of prosperity, of peace with God, and of well-being that is in view, not moral evil, not wickedness. God creates calamity.

He also creates spiritual health for his people.

> You heavens above, rain down righteousness;
>   let the clouds shower it down.
> Let the earth open wide,
>   let salvation spring up,
> let righteousness grow with it;
>   I, the LORD, have created it.[5]

> Create in me a pure heart, O God,
>   And renew a steadfast spirit within me.[6]

In these passages we see God creating righteousness in exactly the same manner that he created the plants and animals on the earth. "Let the earth open wide, let salvation spring up" echoes God's earlier words, "Let the land produce vegetation" and "Let the land produce living creatures." These are spoken in the same jussive voice that God used in the first chapter of Genesis. His work of creating did not end with the arrival of that first Sabbath, but as Jesus explained, "My Father is always at his work to this very day, and I, too, am working."[7]

---

3. Gen. 1:1; Ps. 148:4-5; Gen. 21: 27; Amos 4:13; Isa. 40:26, 43:1, 15; Mal. 2:10; Isa. 43:7; Ps. 148:2-5; Ezek. 28:13-14.
4. Isa. 45:7 NIV.
5. Isa. 45:8 NIV.
6. Ps. 51:10 NIV.
7. John 5:17 NIV.

In fact everything that we see, feel, experience, and hope for is the creation of God. Even the new heaven and new earth are the creation of God.[8] Both past and future are created by God, as he continues to create.

One consistent element in the uses of *bara'* is the directness of God's working. He is not necessarily using means to create. Rather he creates by the force of his own will expressed in commands or in calling things forth. This is how we see God creating in the beginning:

> Praise him, you highest heavens,
>   and you waters above the heavens!
> Let them praise the name of the Lord,
>   for he commanded and they were created.[9]

> Lift your eyes and look to the heavens:
>   Who created all these?
> He who brings out the starry host one by one,
>   and calls them each by name.[10]

And this is how he continues to create:

> But now, this is what the Lord says—
>   he who created you, O Jacob,
>   he who formed you, O Israel:
> "Fear not, for I have redeemed you;
>   I have summoned you by name; you are mine. . . .
> Bring my sons from afar
>   and my daughters from the ends of the earth—
> everyone who is called by my name,
>   whom I created for my glory,
>   whom I formed and made."[11]

Because he is the God who creates by the power of his word, he now creates us anew by calling us by our names and by calling us by his own name. Someday soon he will call us each by a new and secret name at the time when the seeds of this body, having been planted, will bear fruit and we will be dressed in a new flesh.

The greatest distinction of the word "create" (*bara'*) is that it is never used of any creature, but only of God. God alone creates, and when he creates he is doing what only God can do. "To the extent that the OT

---

8. Isa. 65:17.
9. Ps. 148:4-5 NRSV.
10. Isa. 40:26 NIV.
11. Isa. 43:1,6-7 NIV.

reserves the verb exclusively for God, this type of creation has no analogy and is therefore beyond conceptualization."[12] When the word *bara'* is used, there is never any hint of a method or a process. We see just the fact of God's creating, never the how. We do not create on a smaller scale, nor are our art, literature, ingenuity, inventiveness, and imagination able to be compared to God's propensity to *bara'*. Whatever it is that we do, we do not *bara'*; we do not create.

Dorothy Sayers wrote a delightful book, *The Mind of the Maker*, in which she argues that God's image is seen in the fact that humans are creative, that they make things, and especially that they make art.[13] Her argument stems largely from the fact that in the first chapter of Genesis we see God creating; at that point his creative power is all that we know of him. Therefore, she argues, that is the image that must be interpreted in the context of the creation account. Unfortunately, she fails to take into account that Scripture never finds humans to be creative in the sense that God is, and never mentions any person's creating. Curiously, the title of the book is more viable than is the central thesis inside of it; we do find analogy between our making and God's making, but not between God's creating and anything that we do.

The creative power of God has, as stated above, no analogy. We are never given a hint of how God creates, and when he creates there is never a list of ingredients provided so that we may see a process of creation. Rather, God speaks and it is so. God speaks and it begins. God speaks and it is. And it is good.

יָצַר (To Form), Part 1

The verb יָצַר (*yatsar*, to form) carries very different connotations from *bara'*. While both entail the existence of something at the end that did not exist at the beginning, they treat the process of getting from the beginning to the end very differently.

---

12. Ernst Jenni and Claus Westermann, *Theological Lexicon of the Old Testament*, trans. Mark E. Biddle (Peabody, Mass.: Hendrickson Publishers, 1997), 1:255.

13. Dorothy Sayers, *The Mind of the Maker* (San Francisco: Harper Collins, 1979). In this book Sayers deals chiefly with the question of God's image. Though I am convinced she has missed the central idea of God's image, the work remains a delightful book full of insight into the creative process and the workings of the human mind. Sayers follows St. Augustine in seeing myriad trinities within human nature, focusing primarily on the triad of Idea, Energy, and Power. For her this trinity within human creativeness is modeled on the working in creation of the Father, Son, and Holy Spirit. Despite disagreeing with her main premise, I find Sayers's reflections to be extremely thoughtful and provocative.

Thus, while God "commanded and they were created," his forming requires work, time, and material with which to work. The same word in a different form refers both to a potter (a former) and his work of "forming" vessels from clay.

> You turn things upside down,
> as if the potter were thought to be like the clay!
> Shall what is formed say to him who formed it,
> "He did not make me"?
> Can the pot say of the potter,
> "He knows nothing"?[14]

> Does the clay say to the potter,
> "What are you making?"[15]

> "O house of Israel, can I not do with you as this potter does?" declares the LORD. "Like clay in the hand of the potter, so are you in my hand, O house of Israel."[16]

In each of these, the word translated as "potter" is the noun form of the verb that is translated as "to form" or "to fashion" in other places. It could hardly be more different than the word that is usually translated "to create." Not only is *yatsar* used of human activity, while *bara'* is not, but things formed (*yatsar*) are formed from prior material, while things created (*bara'*) are created from nothing at all.

God is said to have formed the mountains, the earth, and the dry land.[17] Interestingly, as Jenni and Westermann have pointed out, he is never said to have formed the sea or the waters.[18] He made them, created them, separated them, filled them, and bounded them, but he is not said to have formed them. The sea is not fixed and firm; it is not shaped as is a clay vessel. Rather, it remains fluid like the clay before it has been through the kiln. Therefore it has not been formed. Forming expresses a transformation from chaos and vagueness to a state of clarity, certainty, and stability. And the sea is indicative of anything but clarity, certainty, and stability.

---

14. Isa. 29:16 NIV.
15. Isa. 45:9 NIV.
16. Jer. 18:6 NIV.
17. Amos 4:13; Isa. 45:18; Jer. 33:2; Ps. 95:5.
18. Jenni and Westermann, *Theological Lexicon of the Old Testament*, 2:567.

עָשָׂה (To Make), Part 1

The verb עָשָׂה (*'asah*, to make) means to make or to do. Throughout the Old Testament it is used for every conceivable type of making. It covers concepts ranging from cows producing milk and trees bearing fruit to a king's throwing a party and Rebekah's preparing food. It extends as far as the idea of butchering a calf.[19] A dead stump may sprout live shoots, and wealth can sprout wings and fly away, or a vine can grow many new branches, and each of these is a use of the word *'asah*.[20]

Clearly *'asah* has a wider range of use than either of the two verbs looked at above. In fact, it can comfortably replace either of the other two, and then some. It even reaches across to cover for the verb "to do." Thus, when God came to accuse the fallen pair, he approached Eve with the words, "What is this you have done (*'asah*)?"[21] And in the next verse he condemns the serpent, "Because you have done (*'asah*) this. . . ." Here we have clearly moved far from the concept of creating and forming and into a different realm.

Those uses of *'asah* that must be translated by some sense of "to make" are rarely difficult to discern. Context differentiates well enough between the two families of meaning to alleviate doubt in most instances. The question that arises is just how to understand the idea of God's "making" anything.

Does the use of this verb intimate a lower act than that delineated by the words "create" and "form"? After all, only one sixth of the instances of *'asah* are attributed to God.[22] The majority refer to acts of people, animals, plants, and even inanimate objects.

Subtle Nuances of the Three Verbs

Why, of these three creation verbs, does God use the one least strongly linked with divine action to propose the creation of humankind? After all, do we not think of this act as the crowning work of creation, as the greatest work God performed prior to the birth of Christ? Is this not the most Godlike of all of God's great works of creation? Why then does God use the word "make" when he suggests the creation of humankind in Genesis 1:26? Would not it have been better to propose, "Let us create"? or "Let us

---

19. Isa. 7:22; Gen. 1:11; Esth. 1:3, 5, 9; Gen. 27:17; Gen. 18:7–8.
20. Job 14:9; Prov. 23:5; Ezek. 17:8.
21. Gen. 3:13 NIV.
22. Jenni and Westermann, *Theological Lexicon of the Old Testament*, 2:946.

form"? At least the word "create" is always and only reserved for works of God, and the word "form" is used of God's works most of the time.

But God does not use words carelessly; we can always be sure that there is no better word to use than the one that God has chosen to use. He does not get tongue-tied and stumble over words, nor does he need to interject "like" or "umm" while he tries to remember the word he wants. Like Dr. Seuss's Horton, he meant what he said, and he said what he meant, Jehovah is accurate one hundred percent.

Jesus once proved a point to the crowds and the Pharisees by pointing out the tense of a verb in their Scriptures: "Now about the dead rising— have you not read in the book of Moses, in the account of the bush, how God said to him, 'I am the God of Abraham, the God of Isaac, and the God of Jacob'? He is not the God of the dead, but of the living. You are badly mistaken!"[23] Jesus is pointing out that by using the present tense when speaking to Moses, God must have meant that the three patriarchs were alive and in his presence. The reason that Jesus could exegete such a massive doctrine from such a minute detail is that God always uses just exactly the right words, although we may miss their beauty and clarity through our dim-wittedness. We may be sure that there is a good reason for God's using the word "make" rather than either of the others, whether or not we can see it.

Besides considering בָּרָא (bara', create), יָצַר (yatsar, form), and עָשָׂה ('asah, make) from the perspective of who is doing them and what is being done, let us ponder a different type of question in regard to each use of the words. Are there any implied concepts that are typically associated with the verbs, and if so, what are they? What are the occasions that call for one or the other? What is the flavor of each verb?

In English we are so familiar with such flavorings of words that we hardly notice them. Subtle nuances differentiate even words that are defined as synonyms. For instance, to punch, smack, hit, or wallop would look little different in a dictionary definition, especially in a bilingual dictionary. The words all carry a meaning of striking with the hand in anger (as well as a variety of other unrelated meanings). Yet although they often could be used interchangeably, there are instances in which one or another is clearly preferable and gives to native English speakers a sense of the action that is decidedly different. We need not spend time detailing these, as the words themselves bring to every native speaker of English various connotations that will supersede any illustrations that I might supply. Consider also the different feelings and flavors of such similar words as

23. Mark 12:26–27 NIV; for parallels see Matt. 22:32 and Luke 20:38.

house and home, or as boy, son, kid, and offspring. Of the latter, consider that any of them could be used to finish the phrase, "That's my. . . ." If either of the first two is true, then so are each of the others. They are very similar and closely related to one another, yet they are as different in usage and subtle implications as they could be.

The subtle differentiations between synonyms give color and texture, flavor and weight or airiness to our speech. This is true of all human languages, not only of English, and it is the part of a language that is the hardest for an outsider to learn. It is the hardest part to present in bilingual dictionaries, yet it is the most expressive part of any language.

בָּרָא (To Create), Part 2

Above we saw that the word "create" can be used only of God. Only God creates. This is one of the word's most distinctive features. We also saw that when God creates there is no indication of method; we see only that what had not been has come to be. The passage from "not being" to "being" is simply expressed as "creation."

While the word "create" is the most exclusive of the three verbs, and also the most masked in mystery, it is nonetheless found in the simplest sentence structures. Most uses of the word occur in simple statements of fact with little else going on in the sentence. Such, for example, is the very first verse: "In the beginning God created the heavens and the earth." There is here no hint of a reason, a method, a tool, or even an evaluation. He just did it. Similarly, when God says, "I will wipe mankind, whom I have created, from the face of the earth," there is simply the statement that he made mankind, with no commentary on the act. Of the forty-one uses of *bara'* in the Hebrew Scriptures, twenty-nine follow this pattern, being simple statements of fact.[24]

In a second use of *bara'*, numbering thirteen cases, the weight of the sentence lies not on the fact being asserted, that such and such was created, but rather on establishing the identity of the God who is either speaking or being spoken of: "This is what God the LORD says—he who created the heavens and stretched them out."[25] The burden of this sentence is not why or how God created; neither is it the fact that he created nor even the

---

24. The numbers given are by my own count and are open to dispute in a few instances. The exact numbers are of little significance other than to establish that one usage has priority over another. The numbers add up to more than forty-one because some sentences fall into both the simple sentence and the naming categories. Those sentences designated as including a sense of purpose are counted only in that category.

25. Isa. 42:5 NIV.

existence of the heavens, but simply that the one being quoted is the same one who stretched them out. It is a method of naming God to say "he who created the heavens."

The third common use of the word *bara'*, to create, occurs in sentences that indicate a purpose for the creation. Thus, when God speaks to Israel of sending them into Canaan to take the land, he promises:

> Before all your people I will do wonders never before done [*bara'*] in any nation in all the world. The people you live among will see how awesome is the work that I, the LORD, will do for you.[26]

He will create wonders in order to amaze the inhabitants of the land of Canaan. In fact, many of the instances in which *bara'* is used in conjunction with a purpose show that the purpose was:

> so that people may see and know,
> may consider and understand,
> that the hand of the LORD has done this,
> that the Holy One of Israel has created it.[27]

Thus, even most of the purpose statements really belong to the category of naming God, of clarifying his identity. Overwhelmingly the word *bara'* has a propensity to delineate the deity, stressing either a *work* that was performed by the deity, that a work was *performed* by the deity, or the *deity* who performed a work. Because *bara'* stresses the incomprehensibility of Yahweh's works, little room is left for commentary. For this reason the sentences are usually short and simple.

יָצַר (To Form), Part 2

Yatsar (to form), associated as it is with its noun form which is translated as "potter," cannot help but have human subjects doing the forming as well as divine subjects. Even so, most (34 of 41) occurrences of the verb "to form" are given with God as the subject. Those with other subjects are always negative in connotation. Consider God's statement, "Before me no god was formed, nor will there be one after me." The one doing the forming is unspecified, for there is no former. Later God promises, "No weapon forged (*yatsar*) against you will prevail."[28] Either the person who forms

---

26. Exod. 34:10 NIV.

27. Isa. 41:20 NIV; see also Ps. 148:5; Num. 16:30; Isa. 43:7; Isa. 45:18.

28. Isa. 43:10; 54:17 NIV. The other instances of *yatsar* being used for subjects other than Yahweh are Ps. 94:20; Isa. 44:9, 10, 12; and Hab. 2:18. In all of these the connotation is decidedly negative.

something is relegated to non-existence, or the thing formed is worthless, or both. Despite this verb's link with a human activity, it seems that only God can get it right. Perhaps the quality of craftsmanship required by *yatsar* is beyond the ability of human workmen. Be that as it may, the vast majority of its uses involve God as the subject and doer of the forming.

In a manner quite distinct from the way "to create" is used, "to form" is only once used in a simple statement of fact without any clear flavoring being put upon it by the surrounding sentence and context. And that use is not about anything actually being formed, but rather sets the time frame, "Before I formed you in the womb."[29] Ignoring that exception, all uses of this verb fall into four categories of nuance: those denoting the method of forming or the substance used in forming, those used to delineate the one who had created, those expressing purpose, and those which evaluate the one forming or the thing formed.

Slightly more than half of the time *yatsar* appears in sentences that seek to establish the identity of one who has formed something rather than seeking to establish the fact of the thing being formed. This usage is similar to the naming use of "to create."

> He who forms the mountains,
> > creates the wind,
> > and reveals his thoughts to man,
> he who turns dawn to darkness,
> > and treads the high places of the earth—
> > the LORD God Almighty is his name.[30]

Unlike the idea of creating, forming often includes mention of the methods and materials used in forming, reflecting its relation to the word translated "potter." God formed *adam* "from the dust," formed beasts "out of the ground," and ordains the days of our lives by writing them in a book.[31] "Can a corrupt throne be allied with you—one that brings on (*yatsar*) misery by its decrees?"[32] Just as we see that the method God uses in ordaining our lives is to write them in a book in advance, so we see that a corrupt ruler's method of forming misery in his subjects is to pass evil laws.

Although the methods and materials of formation are explicitly mentioned in only thirteen of its forty-one uses, the implication is present in all of its uses that there were both materials used and a method or process

29. Jer. 1:5 NIV.
30. Amos 4:13 NIV.
31. Gen. 2:7, 19 NIV; Ps. 139:16.
32. Ps. 94:20 NIV.

followed for forming anything. Thus, when God is described as "he who forms the hearts of all,"[33] we understand that he is not forming these hearts from nothing, but that he is taking hearts that he had previously created—thus they already exist—and is reshaping them in accordance with his desires. We cannot think of formation *ex nihilo* in the same way that we think of creation *ex nihilo*. Formation presupposes some raw material to be worked upon, and some workman to mold that material into a form. When God is said to form the nation of Israel, the idea is present implicitly, even if not explicitly, that he is drawing them from the other peoples by a process. In this sense formation is the polar opposite of creation, which assumes that there is neither method nor material used, but God's mere command, to cause to be that which previously was not.

Less often, the verb "to form" is used in conjunction with the idea of something being formed for a purpose. Leviathan, for example, was formed to frolic in the sea, and the earth was formed to be filled with inhabitants.[34]

A few times *yatsar* is used when either the workman or the product of his work falls under scrutiny.

> All who make (*yatsar*) idols are nothing,
>   and the things they treasure are worthless.
> Those who would speak up for them are blind;
>   they are ignorant, to their own shame.
> Who shapes (*yatsar*) a god and casts an idol,
>   which can profit him nothing? . . .
> The blacksmith takes a tool
>   and works with it in the coals;
> he shapes (*yatsar*) an idol with hammers,
>   he forges it with the might of his arm.
> He gets hungry and loses his strength;
>   he drinks no water and grows faint.[35]

Even these occurrences serve to accentuate the special character of *yatsar*, for these works are subject to ridicule precisely because raw materials and labor are involved in forming idols; therein lies the idols' worthlessness.

So, above all else, whatever contextual nuance the sentence might suggest, the word *yatsar* expresses the making of a new thing from something

---

33. Ps. 33:15 NIV.
34. Ps. 104:26; Isa. 45:18.
35. Isa. 44:9–10, 12 NIV.

that has already been in existence. In this one respect it is the antithesis of *bara'*, of creation.

עָשָׂה (To Make), Part 2

'Asah (to make) exceeds *bara'* and *yatsar* in the uniformity of its usage, and therefore also in the clarity with which it directs our understanding of the acts of God toward his creation. The other two words, as we have seen, are used in a variety of manners and with variation of nuance, sometimes focusing on the person of God who acts, sometimes on an evaluation of the products of formation, sometimes simply setting forth the fact that a creature that had not existed suddenly now does, sometimes focusing on a variety of other matters.

There is, however, virtual unanimity in the usage of *'asah* within the range of its meanings with which we are concerned. What this means is that although *'asah* denotes a variety of meanings, in those cases when it means anything approximating "to make or to create" it displays a surprising consistency of usage.

For our purposes, and in the interest of directness, we will ignore those instances in which *'asah* is best translated by other unrelated verbs, such as "to do" or "to show" (kindness, love, friendship, and so forth). Instead we will focus on just those uses of the verb that relate to our context. Even ignoring the other uses, *'asah* occurs far more often than the other two creation words together. It is extremely common and functions somewhat as an all-purpose word to cover a variety of types of building, constructing, organizing, and preparing.

What is interesting about its uses is that in almost every case the immediate context contains a reason or purpose, a goal or intention for which a thing is being made. The first time that we see the word, in the seventh verse of the Bible, demonstrates this point well. God has just said, "Let there be an expanse between the waters to separate water from water." In no uncertain terms God explains the goal and intention toward which he will work. He wants to separate certain waters from other waters. "So God made (*'asah*) the expanse and separated the water under the expanse from the water above it." God had a purpose, so God made something that fit his purpose.

A few verses later we see that "God made two great lights," and, lest we be in doubt about their use, Moses explains, "the greater light to govern the day and the lesser light to govern the night." Again, he pairs the word *'asah* with the purpose for which the thing is being made. Later, God said,

"It is not good for the man to be alone. I will make (*'asah*). . . ."[36] He saw a lack, so he made something to fill that lack. When the new pair sinned, "they realized they were naked; so they sewed fig leaves together and made coverings for themselves." Again, there was a need, so something was made for the purpose of filling that need.

Time after time we see this pairing: a purpose and a making. God plans to destroy the earth and so tells Noah, "Make yourself an ark . . . ." The inhabitants of Babel wish to build (*'asah*) a tower that will make a name for them so that they will not be scattered.

A single purpose can be extended so that it runs on through a few sentences. For example, when God told Noah to build the ark, he told him the reason at the beginning, but then that purpose holds fast through the next four sentences while God instructs him to make the ark, rooms in it, a roof, decks, and so on. Because this is all being done for the same reason, that reason does not need to be restated in every sentence for it to apply to every command.

Anyone who is following along in a Hebrew Bible will know that I am skipping some uses of the word *'asah*. Often, of course, I skip them because they are better translated by "to do" rather than "to make," but others are less obvious. I have also omitted those cases in which the verb tense is neither present, past, nor future, but past perfect. That is, rather than saying "God made something," the author said, "God had made something." The reason for skipping these is that in most such cases the verb *'asah* is not treated as the central verb of the sentence but only as a subsidiary verb. For instance, "The LORD was grieved that he had made man on the earth, and his heart was filled with pain."[37] Here the subject of the sentence is "LORD," but the verb associated with it is not "had made," but rather, "was grieved." The phrase, "that he had made man" is an explanatory dependent clause functioning as an adverb. Therefore, the verb "had made" in this sentence will not behave as the past tense verb would in a sentence in which it is the controlling verb. Similarly, in the sentence "After forty days Noah opened the window he had made in the ark,"[38] the phrase "he had made" is a dependent adjectival clause. As such, it obviously does not function as a verb and will not behave as if it did.

Therefore it would have been more accurate earlier to say that in almost every case in which *'asah* both means "to make" and is functioning

---

36. Gen. 2:18 NIV.
37. Gen. 6:6 NIV.
38. Gen. 8:6 NIV.

as the subject's verb we will see the purpose of the act of making within the immediate context.

After God brought the Israelites through the sea on dry ground, they saw the Egyptians' corpses rotting on the shore. "And when the Israelites saw the great power the LORD displayed ['asah] against the Egyptians, the people feared the LORD and put their trust in him and in Moses his servant."[39] Taken alone we might think of the people's fear of Jehovah as merely a result of his actions, not as the purpose for them. But when this passage is taken in tandem with such passages as Exodus 7:3-5 and 34:10 we see that "the people feared the LORD" is not just relating the result of God's action, but is in fact telling us why he had done it. He killed the Egyptian army in order to cause his people to fear and trust him and to listen to his servant Moses. Therefore, although it is not apparent in an English translation, the clause "the people feared the LORD and put their trust in him and in Moses his servant" is an expression of the purpose for which God destroyed the Egyptians. This fact is more obvious in the Hebrew because one inherently expects to see a purpose associated with the use of the word 'asah.

How significant could this discussion be? Surely God always has a purpose for anything that he does, regardless of the word used to describe his work. What then is the importance of stressing that a purpose is normally associated with the making of things? The simple fact of there being a purpose has little relevance to our present discussion. What matters to us is not so much that there is a purpose as that that purpose is linked to the word "to make." The word itself seems to assume and include, and even to require, the idea of a reason, a goal, and a purpose in the work of making.

An English word embodying a similar nuance would be "to prepare." This word includes within itself the flavor of a purpose, of an end aimed at. If one prepares a meal, one must see beforehand that the goal is either to eat or to feed someone else. Or one may prepare for an exam, or prepare one's taxes, or prepare for death. But in any case, the idea of a future goal or a planned result is inherent in the word "prepare." A similar nuance does not flavor such English words as "make," "create," or "purchase." This does not mean that we typically make, create, or purchase anything without reasons, just that the words themselves do not include the assumption of purpose.

---

39. Exod. 14:31 NIV.

Likewise, *'asah*—when translatable as a controlling verb meaning "to make"—includes within itself the assumption of a purpose, and that purpose is typically found within the immediate context.

The Three Verbs in Relation to "*Adam*"

In Genesis we see that each of these three creation verbs is used concerning God's creation of *adam*.

> Then God said, "Let us make (*'asah*) man in our image, in our likeness, and let them rule over the fish of the sea and the birds of the air, over the livestock, over all the earth, and over all the creatures that move along the ground."
> So God created (*bara'*) man in his own image,
>   in the image of God he created him;
>   male and female he created them. . . .
>
> The LORD God formed (*yatsar*) the man from the dust of the ground and breathed into his nostrils the breath of life, and the man became a living being.[40]

The last of these says that God formed the man from dust, explaining both from what he made him and how he made him live. This is just what we would expect from what we have observed of the use of the word *yatsar*.

When, in the second case given above, we read that God created man and woman, we understand that God is doing what only God can do. Here we have no hint; we can have no hint as to how or from what God created. Thus, we realize that the phrase "in his own image" can give us no details about the process of creating, for God's creating (whenever it is expressed with the word *bara'*) is always hidden in mystery, and recipes are never given for his hidden work. The phrase "in his own image" must not be taken here as an explanation delineating God's blueprint for creating this man. To take it so would be to violate the veil of secrecy that Scripture holds over God's work of creation. If it were so taken, then this would be the only place in the entire Bible that would give a hint as to how and from what mold God had ever created anything.

Yet that is precisely what is claimed by those who argue that God's image is to be found in any of the traits of humankind, either at our inception or at the present. They say that because we are created in God's image, therefore we are like him by sharing certain of his traits: his holiness, his

---

40. Gen. 1:26, 27; 2:7 NIV.

understanding, his reason, or any of the other traits that we considered in the first chapter. But that is to see this word "create" and to give it the force of the word "form," by making God either the dust from which he formed us or the blueprint according to which he formed us. Does anyone imagine that God sifted through the dirt of himself and picked a few granules of reason, a drop of emotion, a small clod of holiness, and mixed them together to create *adam*?

This may be clarified if we consider again the use of the word "make" given above. When God said, "Let us make man," we are tipped off right away by the word "make" that we should expect that the purpose for which God will make this creature will either be explicit or clearly implicit in the context of the sentence or its immediate environs. Knowing this, the easiest interpretation of God's words is to see the twin phrases "in our image, in our likeness" as the reason, the goal, the purpose for making *adam*. This is how we see the word "make" operate; it is normally paired with the purpose for making.

In order to come to the conclusions about God's image that have been put forward historically by the Roman Catholic and Eastern Orthodox Churches, the Reformed and the Lutheran wings of the church, the Arminians and the Anabaptists, we would have to read both the word "make" and the word "create" as "form." That way we could see, as all of these branches of the church typically have, a delineation of the pattern according to which humans were formed. Whether they are arguing for a purity type of image, a physical image, or an image seen in our attributes and potentials, they all imply that God patterned us after himself. If this is the intent of the passage, then the only word that would have prepared us for such a connotation of the phrase would have been "form."

It is interesting that of the three common creation words, the word "form" is the only one that is never paired with the idea of God's image. Could the reason be that, since it expresses a concept of moving from one state to another, it includes the idea of being made from something prior into something else? Could it be that God wanted no hint of a method or of a material or of a pattern by and from which his image emerged?

Hence, the commonsense reading of the passage lies along the lines, "Let us make mankind in the role of being our image, and for the purpose of displaying our likeness." This reading would instantly cause long lasting squabbles—such as the one over whether the image persists, was destroyed, or was damaged—to melt away like the mirages that they are. If God's image is our purpose and our role, then it may be a purpose that we are fulfilling or not, and a role that we are living in or not, without even hinting at a change in the fact that it is still our purpose and our intended role. The purpose of a screwdriver is unchanged even if I use it as a hammer; how much more does a purpose that God has announced remain unchanged despite my ill performance of that purpose.

Thus the word *'asah* rules out all of the standard theories, for they all posit the image as expressing within individuals a portion of what it means to be God. But if the phrase "in our image" is really revealing not the pattern but the purpose for which humanity is to be created, then we must realize that God will see his purposes through to completion. His purpose will stand. We can reasonably require that any exposition of this passage point toward the whole image of God—involving God's whole being and his whole life—and require that image to encompass all of what it means to be human. Anything less would fall short of the implications inherent in the word "make."

4

Adam

WHILE MANY questions regarding the meaning of God's image have been pondered and debated at length, rarely is the question of the extent of the meaning of the word אָדָם (*adam*) delved into at any appreciable depth. The assumption seems to be that the translations offered in almost all English language Bibles are sufficient to give us full, or at least adequate, understanding. The usual translations of *adam* use the words "man" (e.g., NIV, NASB, KJV, JPS, NWT), "human beings" (e.g., NEB), or "humankind" (e.g., NRSV).

But each of these words is horrendously vague, especially when we consider that this verse is integral to our understanding of what those words themselves will mean. When the anthropological question "What does it mean to be human?" is brought up, this is one of the first texts to which any theologian will turn in answering. There is an old rule that a word should never be used in its own definition, but here we have the meaning of the words in question dependent on the meaning we apply to them in the definitive text.

The difficulty is analogous to making the request—if one can assume such a request being voiced completely apart from any preexisting context—"Tell me your story." Void of any context or setting, from whom could one expect an answer? From the sky? From the breeze in one's hair? Will the daffodils answer us? Even if we were to get an answer the length of *Uncle Tom's Cabin*, but lack an answer to the fundamental question of whose life story was being told, we would learn little. Whose story would we have heard?

The Extent of "*adam*"

Uncle Tom's Cabin is a useful example in this case, for whose story did Harriet Beecher Stowe detail in that book? Was it Tom's story? Or was it Eliza's story? If a reporter had gone in search of the "real" Uncle Tom there would have been no Tom to find. No individual's life ever corresponded in very great detail to the lives portrayed in that book. Instead of telling an individual's story, Mrs. Stowe poured the lives and loves, the hurts and dreams of all of the American slaves into those few characters. So once we learn the life stories of Tom and Eliza, we do not know the stories of Tom and Eliza, but rather we know something about the corporate story of the American slave. By this means we have established a context for the answer to our question, and in this case the context is not an individual life, but rather countless lives that are being considered together as a unity, as a whole, as incorporated into a single story that tells all of their stories while telling the story of none of them as individuals.

In Stowe's book we are brought face to face with one of the fundamental questions of humanity: Is human history the collected stories of many individuals, or is there one unified story that encompasses a great multitude? Whom does Scripture declare to be the image of God, individual human beings or humanity considered as a whole? Or dare we dichotomize and set these two at odds? Are they fundamentally unmixable, as are envy and shalom, and unable to both be true, or could they in fact each depend upon the other in a symbiotic relationship?

The word we must examine in order to answer these questions is "*adam*," which is, of course, the same word as is used for the first man, Adam. It functions in Hebrew both as a generic, translated "man/mankind/humankind," or as a proper name, transliterated "Adam." At first glance, therefore, we might wonder whether we ought to see here a proposal to make just one particular individual as God's image. If our eyes continue through the rest of the sentence, however, we see that more is in view than just an individual: "Let Us make man in Our image, according to Our likeness; and let *them* rule. . . ."[1] This plural (my italics) instantly denies us the possibility of seeing in these words a single individual man as the focus of God's attention, or at least as the sole focus of God's attention. The same result occurs in the next verse, in which "*adam*" is both "male and female," who are then called by the plural "them."[2] This plurality is reiterated at the beginning of the genealogies in chapter 5, "Male and female he created them, and he blessed them and named them 'Humankind' when they

---

1. Gen. 1:26 NASB.

2. The plural "them" in these two verses should be enough to dispel the notion that Adam the individual was a hermaphrodite until God removed the woman from his body while he slept, but, alas, a quick search on the Internet will show that this teaching is quite common. The fact that *adam* is "male and female" should rather lead us to understand that *adam* has reference to more than an individual.

were created."³ The word translated "Humankind" here is the same word "*adam*" that was used in 1:26.

In the absence of any constraining contextual clues, the word אָדָם (*adam*) is fully able to carry any of at least three distinct meanings: Adam, the proper name of the first human; a particular individual (as in "a person" or "the person"); or humanity taken *en toto* (as distinct from God and the rest of creation).⁴ And occasionally *adam* is used in a fourth sense to distinguish a man from a woman, although that duty is normally left to the word אִישׁ (*ish*, here in Genesis 5:2 meaning "man or male"). Furthermore, the presence or absence of the definite article with *adam* does not clearly distinguish which meaning is intended. The word can be used as a proper name either with or without the definite article. Thus Genesis 4:1, "*the* Adam knew his wife," and 4:25, "Adam knew his wife again," are both uses of the word as Adam's proper name. "This fluidity between the definite and indefinite form makes it difficult to know when the personal name 'Adam' is first mentioned (LXX 2:16; AV 2:19; RV and RSV 3:17; TEV 3:20; NEB 3:21)."⁵

The ambiguity of the word *adam* becomes tellingly significant when we consider the change in number voiced by God when he comes to the creation of humankind. Please note that we are here going to consider the relationship between the number (in the sense of singulars and plurals) in which God calls the creatures into existence and the number in which God proposes to create humankind. This shift in number reflects a difference in the manner in which God *speaks* of us compared to how he speaks of the other creatures. This point must not be confused with the discussion that will follow a few paragraphs later concerning the "strange numbers" that are used, not *by* God per se, but *about* God. The first chapter of the Bible is filled brim full of numbers, and they are vital to the present discussion in more than one way.

As was said, the ambiguity here as to which meaning should be applied to the word *adam* emphasizes the significance of contextual clues such as the dramatic shift in numbers voiced by God when it comes to the creation of humans. The other living creatures were all called forth in the plural, as groups of individuals: plants yielding seed, fruit trees, swarms of living creatures, birds, sea monsters, cattle, creeping things, and wild animals. Humankind, however, was set out from the very beginning as a

---

3. Gen. 5:2 NRSV.

4. Gordon J. Wenham, *Genesis*, vol. 1, *One Through Fifteen* (Waco, Texas: Word Books, 1987), p. 32.

5. Ibid.

unit, a singular body. This singular *adam* as opposed to the plural *adamah* is the difference between "humankind" and "humans." While nearly all modern translators and expositors see the concept of all humanity in this reference to *adam*, it is not often noted that this humanity is being considered as a single living body, a single group, rather than a plural collection of individuals.

The great family of humanity, the body of Adam, all came through Adam, the headwaters from which we flow as a single river physically, and our head spiritually from whom we inherit our contrary and sinful nature.[6] He is our head and we were seen in him at creation, just as Levi already lived in his ancestor Abraham when Abraham paid the tithe to Melchizedek.[7] Therefore, God created us all when he created Adam. We are the body of Adam, the filling out of humankind, in much the same way that the church is called the body of Christ. God called forth humanity in the singular, and then expounds that this single body is comprised of distinct units, "male and female," and "them."

Just as God made humankind (singular) in his image (singular), so also the New Testament concept of the church as the body of Christ insists that because there is but one Christ there is but one body. And that one body is being conformed to his one image.[8]

"Adam" and *"Ish"*

The collective or unitary understanding of *adam* is buttressed by the fact that *adam* is not the only Hebrew word commonly translated as "man." Layers of ambiguity are added to the text by the decision of translators to render both *adam* and *ish* using the same English word "man." Thus, what the Hebrew author chose to distinguish, the English translators have chosen to unite. The difference between the two is similar to the difference between the English words "person" and "man." While *ish* distinguishes male humans (*ish*) from female humans (*ishshah*), *adam* is not generally used to make such a distinction. Use of *adam* serves rather to distinguish between humankind and animalkind.

Thus, we do not find the word *ish* used until there is an *ishshah* from which to distinguish him:

---

6. Consider Gen. 3:20; Luke 3:38; 1 Cor. 15:22; Rom. 5:15.
7. Heb. 7:9-10.
8. 1 Cor. 10:16-17; Col. 3:9-12.

And the Lord God fashioned the rib that He had taken from the *adam* into a *ishshah*; and He brought her to the *adam*. Then the *adam* said,
> "This one at last
> Is bone of my bones
> And flesh of my flesh.
> This one shall be called *ishshah*,
> For from *ish* was she taken."

Hence a *ish* leaves his father and mother and clings to his *ishshah*, so that they become one flesh.[9]

The proposal to make *adam* in God's image clearly was neither a proposal to make only the male in God's image nor a proposal to make only a single individual in God's image. We again are left with the idea that God was proposing to make for his image an entire species, the species called *adam*.

As soon as we recognize that in Genesis 1:26 God proposed to do a work involving the entire human race together, a few things begin to press in on our minds. First, we realize that the full picture of what God means by his image will not become apparent if we look only at some particular part or individual. When doing a jigsaw puzzle, we cannot see the picture by looking at any single piece. Just so, God's image, which he is forming, will not be visible if we look solely at individuals. Even looking at many individual pieces of this complex puzzle to see what each has in common with God will give us only the most elementary, inadequate, and reductionist ideas of what could be their common goal. The full meaning of God's image is not visible from within the puzzle, from within the framework of history, but must be seen from the vantage point of the puzzle maker.

Second, God's image must be understood eschatologically, as the assignment imposed at our creation and the goal toward which human history is moving (not by its own volition, but by God's overarching providence). Until all *adam*, or humankind, is in the picture, God's image will not be complete. God is still in the process of forming his image, and the grand flow of human history is inevitably (because he is sovereignly in control of it) moving toward the fullness of that image. Thus, the meaningless (from our perspective) suffering of life on earth will ultimately be

---

9. Gen. 2:22-24 JPS. The words "man," "woman," and "wife" have been replaced with transliterations of the Hebrew roots which they translate to show how the roots change with the context although the English does not reflect the variance.

found to be filled with meaning when we see the glory of what God has formed in us.

Similarly, it is entirely possible that not all are *adam* who are descended from Adam. Just as there are many within the covenant community of Israel who are not of the family that God is welcoming into his rest, so also it is at least possible that not all within the covenant community of Adam are included in God's image. Indeed, the coming of a "second Adam" would seem to lead us in this direction. Each of these possibilities will be considered more intently in the last five chapters.

Although God's image, as will be seen more clearly in the final chapters, must be understood eschatologically as developing (or progressing in stages) and as having its ultimate fulfillment in the future celebration of Jesus' salvation, we must not think that therefore God's image pertains only to the elect. Both the Old Testament and the New make clear that all humanity shares in this image. For instance, Genesis 9:6 declares that we are not permitted to murder any human, for all are created in God's image. And James chastises his readers for cursing "those who are made in the likeness of God."[10] The word here translated "those" is the Greek word ανθρωπους (*anthrōpous*), which means "men" or "people." That it has reference to more than the body of believers becomes clear when read in the context of the passage, for James is continually calling his readers αδελφοι (*adelphoi*, brothers). The non-familial term *anthrōpous*, "people," stands out coldly in contrast to James's warm manner of addressing those whom he sees as being within the fellowship. Therefore, we must let neither the eschatological implications of God's image nor the universality of that image obscure the other. Every human being who ever has existed or ever will exist is included, even Caiaphas and Hitler, and the full working out of that image will not be completed until history has run its course and we see Jesus face to face.

Unless the reader has been lulled to sleep, the last two paragraphs will likely grate on each other like fingernails on a chalkboard. Do they not seem to utterly contradict each other? And yet in reality there is no difficulty between them, for being a covenant member and being a covenant keeper are two entirely different things. Many who are created to display God's likeness will never fulfill that role, just as many who are circumcised into Abraham are not true Israel, and many who are baptized are not ultimately found to be "in Christ," and many who say "I do" do not fulfill the role of husband or wife. To be placed into a covenant relationship and to live in that covenant are entirely different matters. While we cannot do

---

10. James 3:9 NRSV.

the latter without the first being accomplished, we find it all too easy to be in but not of covenants. That is our pathetic nature as fallen *adam*; we are covenant breakers.

But let us consider the implications of the word *adam* in another light.

The Numbers Get Strange

Among the most intriguing things to ponder in the first chapter of the Bible are the oddities of the numbers. The grammar does not work. From the opening line, "In the beginning God created," we sense a tension. The word that we so blandly translate as "God" is אֱלֹהִים (*elohim*), a word that is plural in form. Yet the verb translated "created" calls for a singular subject doing this creating. In English this difficulty could be illustrated by the translation "In the beginning the Gods (third person plural) creates (third person singular)."

As we move through the chapter we see the English introduction to each new day of creation, "God said," or "And God said," or "Then God said." In each instance we have the plural word *elohim* translated rather blandly by our all-purpose deity term "God." Again the verbs do not agree with the subjects, and to illustrate the grammatical difficulty we could translate each of these as "Then the Gods (third person plural) says (third person singular)."

But each of these translations would create difficulties of its own, and they are best left out of the standard translations. Nevertheless we are left with the question, "Did Moses understand grammar? Why did he mess up so badly in this chapter?" Or is it really an error?

A detailed analysis of all of the arguments would take us far afield from the topic at hand. Instead let us quote Gordon Wenham, who rightly noted that the use of "*elohim*" is "plural in form but singular in meaning."[11] Here it would seem that we have the scholarly version of the parent at bedtime who replies to incessant questions with the answer, "Go to bed now, and ask me again in the morning." But Wenham's answer is brilliant, for it tells us how to handle the difficulty without trying to explain away the difficultness of the difficulty, and such puzzles should not be explained away. The difficulty remains and must remain, even if we see this, as I do, as a reference to the community of the Trinity.

I find it interesting that the same difficulties of grammar that are displayed in this chapter are encountered by theologians trying to do justice

---

11. Wenham, *Genesis*, vol. 1, *One Through Fifteen*, p. 14.

to the biblical teachings about the three persons who are the one God. In this context Millard Erickson has been driven to use such "logically odd language" as "He are three" and "They is one."[12] The problem encountered by following grammar rules when speaking of the Trinity is that inevitably either the threeness or the oneness will be emphasized. By ignoring grammar, the difficulty of equally emphasizing both simultaneously is not obscured, but rather is highlighted; thus the tension inherent in the text is preserved.

This "logically odd language" is what we encounter in the creation story's references to God, masked though the oddness may be in our common English translations. (Incidentally, the same problem exists in English translations of the last book of the Bible, in which the apostle John intentionally ran afoul of grammarians but our helpful translators have generally "fixed" his "errors.")

But let us turn to verse 26 which reads, "Let Us make man in Our image, according to Our likeness; and let them rule. . . ."[13] Here, as with the references to the Godhead, is a verb that does not agree in number with its referent; the plural verb (let them rule) clearly refers to the singular noun "man." And simply translating *adam* as "mankind" will not help, except in English. The Hebrew verb still does not agree with its noun.

What does this noun/verb disagreement mean in reference to humanity? Are we also a trinity? While we are not warranted to go that far, we can at least say that God is here showing that he sees us both as a collective body (by the singular *adam* or "man") and as individuals (by the plural "let them rule"). Both the collective sense and the individual sense are reinforced by the next verse, "God created man in His own image, in the image of God He created him; male and female He created them."[14] As was shown above, the singular word *adam* as it is used here does not, and indeed cannot, have reference to an individual, but rather refers to a group that is considered as a whole and is hence one unit. If it were a group considered as individuals, it would be plural; if it were simply an individual, it could not be paired with the plural "let them rule."

In this word *adam* God refers simultaneously to individuals and to all of all humanity considered as a single body. We see that *adam* is one; *adam* is two; *adam* is many.

---

12. Millard J. Erickson, *God in Three Persons: A Contemporary Interpretation of the Trinity* (Grand Rapids: Baker, 1995), p. 270; quoted in Ralph A. Smith, *Paradox and Truth* (Moscow, Idaho: Canon Press, 2002), pp. 48–49.

13. Gen. 1:26 NASB.

14. Gen. 1:27 NASB.

Adam

The Numbers Get Stranger

If God sees us both as a collective body, which we may term humanity or humankind, and as individuals, what implications should we draw?

Again we will turn to the fact that the numbers were not working grammatically in chapter 1 even before verse 26 about the creation of humanity. God's numbers did not add up either. Why not? Is there an implicit connection between the problems with God's numbers and with ours?

To answer the second question first, you be the judge. When twenty-five subject/verb disagreements concerning God are immediately followed by a couple of subject/verb disagreements concerning humanity, do you think that there might be a connection? Bear in mind that grammar was, if anything, more important in the Hebrew language than it is in English, for Hebrew often has implied subjects in which the verb formation contains or implies the subject. Disagreement would grate on the Hebrew ear just as much as it grates on ours. I think that the connection, once recognized, is obvious.

If the answer to our number difficulty lies in the Trinitarian union, then we must ask how that union works. How do God's grammatical difficulties (as they are seen in this creation chapter) get answered in the Trinity?

Here we come home to the center of our Christian faith, the ground of all truth, the mystery of God. Who is God? Who are God? How many are God? How many is God?

"God is one." So cries Israel's *shma*,[15] and Christianity shouts a loud "Amen!" But Christianity dares name this one God: He is the Father, and he is the Son, and he is the Holy Spirit. He is three, and one. These three are absolutely distinct and individual, else it would be worse than play-acting (Jesus called the Pharisees play actors, and it was not a compliment) when Jesus converses with his Father, or when the Father commands his Son, or when Jesus sends his Spirit. Threeness is absolutely nonnegotiable. But then so is oneness.[16]

Do we therefore play word games and mind games, trying to get a mental picture that will satisfy us that we are not asserting oneness and

---

15. Deut. 6:4 NASB: "Hear, O Israel! The LORD is our God, the LORD is one!"

16. This section on the Trinity is indebted to three books by Ralph Smith, *Paradox and Truth*, *Eternal Covenant*, and *Trinity and Reality* (Moscow, Idaho: Canon Press, 2002, 2003, and 2004, respectively).

threeness of just the same thing?[17] No, for that is just what we are asserting. Jesus is God. God is one. The Father is God. God is one. The Spirit is God. God is one. The Trinity is God. God is one. Jesus, the Father, the Holy Spirit; God is also three.

The Father is no less God than is the Trinity. When God-with-us walked the earth, he was no less God than is the Godhead on the throne. They are not parts of God, as if God were divisible; they each are the fullness of God. We must maintain that they are three persons and one person, that each is God and all together is neither more nor less of God.

But here the mathematics do not compute.

$$\begin{array}{r} \text{One God} \\ \text{One God} \\ + \underline{\text{One God}} \\ \text{One God} \end{array}$$

$$\begin{array}{r} \text{One Person} \\ \text{One Person} \\ + \underline{\text{One Person}} \\ \text{One Person} \end{array}$$

Such numbers would lead us to question our sanity in believing them if it were not that both the parts above the lines and the parts below are so clearly attested in Scripture. This is not the place for a defense of Trinitarianism, and anyway that defense has been made from Scripture enough times that any searcher will easily find a dozen well constructed arguments for the facts in our addition problems above. Therefore, we will move on.

Making Trinitarian Math Work

In his high priestly prayer of John 17, Jesus makes a number of mathematically puzzling statements and petitions, and these may help clear up for us both the difficulty with the Trinitarian math and the logically odd math of the numbers relating to *adam*. Let us look at a few sentences of Jesus' prayer.

> Holy Father, protect them by the power of your name—the name you gave me—so that they may be one as we are one. . . .

---

17. Some word pictures for the Trinity are familiar: ice, liquid, steam, but all one water; or father, son, and brother, but all one man. These analogies, however, all end in heresy, usually (as in the two just mentioned) in the heresy of modalism or of saying that the three persons are not distinct but are merely different ways God shows himself to us.

> I pray also for those who will believe in me through their message, that all of them may be one, Father, just as you are in me and I am in you. May they also be in us so that the world may believe that you have sent me. I have given them the glory that you gave me, that they may be one as we are one: I in them and you in me. May they be brought to complete unity to let the world know that you sent me and have loved them even as you have loved me.[18]

Here we hear Jesus referring to himself and his Father as "one," and even asking that we, his disciples throughout the ages, would be made "one" in a similar fashion. That word "as," "that they may be one *as* we are one," means that there is at least an analogical, if not a definitive, connection between the oneness of Father and Son and the oneness of humans. Our unity will resemble their unity; at least, it will if Jesus' prayer on the night before his crucifixion was heard and answered by his Father.

But Jesus' words go much further than this. So far we are only up to the level of difficult math, that two are one and that many are one. What is the unifier that makes them one? What is the unifier that will make us one?

The essence of Jesus' answer can be summed up with one word: indwelling. Notice how Jesus assumes a parallel between our unity and the mutual indwelling between himself and his Father. He prays, "that all of them may be one, Father, *just as* you are in me and I am in you." That "just as" means that our human unity is to resemble the deity's unity, which Jesus expresses as a mutual indwelling.

This of course begs the question of indwelling: just how in is in? What does Jesus mean when he says that the Father is in him and he is in the Father? The answer is apparent in its result. They are in each other such that they are a unity; they are one. They are so in each other that Jesus was able to say, "If you have seen me, you have seen the Father."[19] Such an indwelling is absolute and without limit. Where the Father is, there the Son and the Spirit are in and through him. Where the Son is, there the Spirit and the Father are in and through him. Where the Spirit is, there the Father and Son are also.

It is not only on earth that Jesus does nothing on his own, but only what his Father wills him to do; rather, he follows his Father's will on earth because that is and has been Jesus' pattern of behavior throughout eternity. Jesus did not come to earth and only then suddenly begin to play a role that was vastly different than his role had been before he descended. He in whom there is no shadow of turning did not suddenly turn over a new

---

18. John 17:11, 20–23 NIV.
19. John 14:9 CEV.

leaf to become subservient, when he had been otherwise for eternity past. "I delight to do thy will, O my God"[20] were words to which his lips had been accustomed since before the creation of the world and to which they will remain accustomed by constant use for ages to come. Jesus was never heard to pray, "Father, restore me to the place that I had when I was with you so that I won't have to be bothered with obeying you."

If we were to trace this concept throughout the Scriptures we would find that every thought and motive in Jesus' heart is to please his Father, to glorify his Father, to bring honor to his Father. To this end Jesus, through his Spirit, searches the depths of his Father's heart, to mine from there treasures which will add to the honor of his Father.

The Father reciprocates fully, never using Jesus just to add to his own honor but always directing the Son unto the uplifting and edification of the Son. Just one case in point: the Father planned the creation, fall, redemption, and glorification of humanity in order to exalt Jesus "far above all rule and authority, power and dominion, and every title that can be given, not only in the present age but also in the one to come."[21] The Father and the Son are not self-seeking, but always seek to exalt the other. If we had time and space, all of these things could be shown of the Holy Spirit also, that he seeks to display the glories of the Father and the Son and that they also work for the Spirit's glory. But this is not a treatise on the nature of the Trinity, so we must curtail this part of the discussion, though more will be said in a later chapter.

Before moving on we must see clearly that it is in this putting aside of self and seeking the glorification of the other that the three actually become/remain one.[22] Throughout all of eternity Jesus has thought not about raising himself up but rather about raising up the other members of the Trinity. In so doing, he searches the hearts and minds of the others, and it is his will to please them, even while it is their will to please him. As they each seek to know the others and to glorify the others—and as they each remain completely open to the probing of the others; not only giving but also receiving; not only asking but also answering; each of them

---

20. Ps. 40:8 KJV; see also Heb. 10:7.

21. Eph. 1:21 NIV.

22. Once again we run into the inevitable frailty of human language when dealing with the Godhead. It is foolish to say "the three become one," for that implies that at one time they were not one. This is false. But language fails me as to how to convey the concept without becoming awkward in expression. Should I say, "the three is one," or "the three be one"? I am comforted that biblical language becomes awkward at points when God is speaking of himself: "Before Abraham was, I am," and "I am that I am."

outwardly motivated, but that outward looking being fully reciprocated—they show themselves to be fully and beautifully intertwined. Thus, when we see Jesus we see him continually searching the mind of the Father and of the Spirit and submitting himself for the Father's glory to the will of the Father, which in its turn is only focused on the further manifestation of the glory of the Son and the Spirit.

When we contemplate this relationship that Jesus referred to as "I in you and you in me," we discover that we will never see more of the Father than when we look at Jesus, for the Father is constantly in Jesus and Jesus is constantly in the Father. Nor will we ever see more of Jesus than we will in the Spirit whom Jesus sent, for they indwell each other fully and continually. Thus any individual member of the Trinity is the whole Trinity, and the whole of the Trinity is no more than any part of the Trinity, so the sum of the three is One. Each is One and all is One. God is One.

What Trinitarian Math Means to Us

How does their unity relate to us mere mortals? Perhaps it should frighten us, for the testimony of Scripture, from the Genesis 1 confusion of our numbers to Jesus' high priestly prayer, seems to be that we are meant to display the same qualities of impassioned other-seeking as the members of the Godhead do, and to do so to such a degree that we also begin to indwell each other and become one. For us who have drunk so long from the individualistic cistern, the idea of leaving ourselves open to being probed by others is likely just as unimaginable as is the idea of submitting our will to the will of others for their good.

In this context we see how truly radical is the idea that we must "do nothing out of selfish ambition or vain conceit, but in humility consider others better than [our]selves."[23] We are not to act from self-centered motivations, just as Jesus does not seek his own but rather his Father's glory. We are to follow Jesus in putting away our own lives and all of our passions and hopes and plans for self-aggrandizement, and to humbly follow him down the road of submission to the Father's will for the gain of others. Self-seeking should be as foreign to us as it is to the members of the Godhead. In a covenant community, such as is the Trinity, there is no danger in loving others to the exclusion of ourselves, for each other member of the covenant community has our interests at heart and searches us for our good.

23. Phil. 2:3 NIV.

In this way we are able to see what Paul could mean by such words as "I no longer live, but Christ lives in me."[24] Paul has set his life aside; it is now hidden in Christ and is no longer Paul's concern. Rather, his concern is now all and only to do the will of Jesus; therefore, Christ is living and acting in Paul. Paul's life emulates (imperfectly, to be sure, but vitally nonetheless) the relationship between the individual members of the Trinity. This is the relationship that we each must emulate with respect to Jesus, and also with respect to each other. Jesus prayed not only that we would be in him (although that was part of his prayer), but that we also would be one with each other.

All of this is clearly laid out in Paul's letter to the Philippians:

> Make my joy complete by being like-minded, having the same love, being one in spirit and purpose. Do nothing out of selfish ambition or vain conceit, but in humility consider others better than yourselves. Each of you should look not only to your own interests, but also to the interests of others.
>
> Your attitude should be the same as that of Christ Jesus:
>
>> Who, being in very nature God,
>>   did not consider equality with God something to be grasped,
>> but made himself nothing,
>>   taking the very nature of a servant,
>>   being made in human likeness.
>> And being found in appearance as a man,
>>   he humbled himself
>>   and became obedient to death—even death on a cross!
>> Therefore God exalted him to the highest place
>>   and gave him the name that is above every name,
>> that at the name of Jesus every knee should bow,
>>   in heaven and on earth and under the earth,
>> and every tongue confess that Jesus Christ is Lord,
>>   to the glory of God the Father.[25]

Our unity is to be built on self-sacrifice, just as was Jesus' relation to the Father, and in the end our self-sacrifice will be found to be in our own best self-interest. That self-interest, however, is not a mercenary motivation but rather the gift of a loving God who has been displaying this same self-giving love toward us all the time. He is not requiring of us anything that he has not already and continually done himself.

---

24. Gal. 2:20 NIV.
25. Phil. 2:2–11 NIV.

Such a path, fully followed, would end both in our being one *and* in our being individuals. In fact, we would be more fully individuals than we now are, for rather than just one seeking my fulfillment there would be numberless others also seeking it. But can this path be followed? Are we humans able to indwell each other, to set our own wills aside for the good of others in the same way that the members of the Trinity do?

Before answering in the negative, let us remember that in the creation God considered us to be both individuals and a collective unit. Remember that Jesus prayed that we would be a unit just as he and his Father are a unit. Remember that we are commanded both by Jesus and by Paul to become a unit through self-denying love. Finally, remember that the church is called the one body of the one Christ. If the analysis that has been given of the number difficulties in the first chapter of Genesis is valid, then the door is barred against our taking Jesus' words when he prayed that we would be one either as merely figurative or as wholly future. They are no more figurative for us than they are for the Trinity, and they are no more limited to the future for us than they are for the Trinity. The question is not "Can we?" but rather, "Will we?"

5

In the Role of God's Image

OFTEN IN this world it is the smallest things that have the greatest effects. I remember as a boy riding in a car with my mother and brother. A bee flew in the window and began buzzing around my sleeping brother. Concerned lest he be stung, my mother began shooing it toward the window. Moments later, we were bumping and jolting down into a ditch from which we were unable to remove the car until we were pulled out by a truck. The smallest creature in the car, the bee, had been able to alter the course of the car and its passengers from that intended by the three humans. And we three humans indubitably thought ourselves to be much wiser, stronger, and more valuable than that little bee.

Similarly, sometimes it can be the smallest words that determine the whole direction of a sentence. Consider the following:

> Robin loped through the gate with a sword at his side.

> Robin loped through the gate with a sword in his side.

These pictures are nearly opposites. Prepositions are often the smallest members of a sentence, but they wield great power over its direction. With this in mind, let us consider the prepositions in the sentence at hand.

In the Role Of

The two prepositions, ב (*b-*) and כ (*k-*), when prefixed to nouns, are commonly translated by "in" or "by" and by "as" or "like" respectively.[1] In Genesis 1:26 and 1:27 they are usually translated this way. Thus we find "in the image of God" and "according to our likeness," or similar wording, in most translations. Both prepositions, however, are also able to carry

---

1. Gordon J. Wenham, *Genesis*, vol. 1, *One Through Fifteen* (Waco, Texas: Word Books, 1987), p. 28.

In the Role of God's Image

the closely related connotation of "as" or "in the capacity or role of."[2] For example:

> Exodus 6:3: "I appeared to Abraham, Isaac, and Jacob בְּ (as, in the capacity of) El-Shaddai."
>
> Deuteronomy 28:68: "You shall offer yourselves for sale to your enemies בְּ (as, in the role of) male and female slaves."
>
> Genesis 1:14: "let them be בְּ (for the purpose/role of) signs and for seasons."
>
> Genesis 6:21: "it shall serve בְּ (to serve as, so that it may function as) food for you."

Could we translate any of these with the words "in" or "according to"?

Abraham Kuyper made this same point by examining a selection of uses of the preposition בְּ which he calls by its transliteration "B."

> We find the same result in Lev. xvii. 11: "The life of the flesh is in the blood, and I have given it to you upon the altar, to make an atonement for your souls; for it is the blood that maketh an atonement for the soul." Here the same preposition "B" occurs. In the Hebrew it reads: "Banefesh" (בַּנֶּפֶשׁ), which was translated *"for* the soul." It would be absurd to render it: "*in* the soul"; for the blood does not come *in* the soul, nor does the atonement take place in the soul, but on the altar. Here we have also a comparison (substitution). The blood is *as* the soul, *represents* the soul in the atonement, takes the place of the soul.[3]
>
> Again, Psalm xxxv. 2 reads: "Take hold of shield and buckler and stand up for mine help." "Stand up *in* my help" makes no sense. The thought allows no other translation than this: "Stand up so that Thou be my help;" or, "Stand up *as* my help"; or, as the Authorized Version has it: "Stand up *for* my help."[4]

From these and many other instances we may see that the prepositions commonly translated by "in" and "after" in Genesis 1:26-27 are elsewhere quite often entirely unable to support such translations. The idea carried by these prepositions often is that of existing for or being claimed for a purpose, existing with a goal, or existing with a role to play out. The

---

2. See the arguments offered by H. Wildberger, D. J. A. Clines, and W. Gross summarized in Wenham, p. 29.

3. Abraham Kuyper, *The Work of the Holy Spirit*, trans. Henri De Vries (Grand Rapids: Eerdmans, 1979), pp. 238-39.

4. Ibid., p. 238.

blood of the altar is claimed *for the purpose of* substitution and atonement. The Israelites will offer themselves *in the role of* slaves. The Lord is begged to *play the role of* a buckler and shield, so as to defend the psalmist.

These are the two prepositions prefixed onto "image" and "likeness": thus we have ב / image and כ / likeness. How can we know which translation—"in" and "according to," or "in the role of" and "for the purpose of"—is more likely to be correct in Genesis 1:26-27?

It is interesting that the import of ב (*b-*) and כ (*k-*) becomes more nearly synonymous in the set "in the role of/for the purpose of," or more simply "as/for," than in the "in/after" schema. This synonymity should be expected in light of Genesis 5:3 in which the same prepositions are united with the same nouns, but in reverse pairing. Thus "ב (*b-*) / image" becomes "ב (*b-*) / likeness" and "כ (*k-*) / likeness" becomes "כ (*k-*) / image." Because this reversal does not seem even to hint at a different treatment of either the prepositions or the nouns, their reversal strongly indicates that the two prepositions are interchangeable in the sense in which they are used. Such easy interchangeability leans sharply away from the common "in/after" translations, which are not easily interchanged, and toward the "in the role of/for the purpose of" translations.

There are at least five significant differences between the implications of understanding these prepositions as "in the role of/in the capacity of/for the purpose of" and understanding them to mean "in/after." One, as has already been mentioned, is the interchangeability of the two prepositions when they are used in Genesis 5:3.

Second, "in the role of" does not imply either a past or present perfection or achievement of that image in the manner that the traditional translation does. This disparity between calling and achievement is in keeping with biblical theology and all evidence. Indeed, if we were currently God's image in the fullest sense of the term, what would be so special about calling Jesus "the express image" of God?[5]

Third, the "role" understanding suggests an eschatological interpretation which we see evidenced in the New Testament doctrine of saints progressively becoming conformed to the image of Christ. The idea that history is moving from immaturity toward maturity, and that humanity is likewise being brought from immaturity toward maturity, is not solely a New Testament notion. It is to be found in the Hebrew Scriptures as well. Terms such as "the day of the Lord," "fullness of time," and "last days" demonstrate that the Hebrew notion of time was based on moving toward a fulfillment. In fact, the very idea of a particular moment of creation

---

5. Heb. 1:3 KJV.

requires an eschatological doctrine of history. Similarly, the stress on the coming of one who would "bruise" the serpent's head,[6] redeem Israel, and set the captives free, reminds us that humans were to be likewise brought toward a fulfillment. This eschatological understanding is utterly absent from the traditional translations of these prepositions, but is everywhere present in Scripture. In fact, the traditional "*in* the image" translation lends itself to a "had something—lost it—hope to regain it" view of history which is emphatically subbiblical.

Fourth, the prepositions "in" and "after" allow for a reading in which only a fraction of our personhood is involved in this image and only a fraction of God is imaged. This is, in fact, the reading that has almost exclusively been used by theologians and commentators. As was seen earlier, whether it be the intellectual part of humanity or our physical aspect or human moral purity that is held to constitute God's image, it is always just a small part of our humanness and a small part of God that is in view. For example, in Jonathan Edwards's phrase, the image of God becomes merely "those faculties and principles of nature whereby [we are] capable of moral agency."[7] Such compartmentalizing of the human person is foreign to biblical anthropology which invariably sees humans either as whole individuals or as members of groups. Understanding these prepositions to mean "in the role of/in the capacity of/for the purpose of," or more simply "as/for," eliminates the possibility of reading the image of God as being a partial mirroring.

Fifth, and most significant, is the idea that this preposition must "agree" with the rest of the sentence. Just as the subject and verb must agree in a sentence, being either both singular or both plural, and a pronoun must agree with its antecedent, so also these prepositions must agree with the verb "to make" that accompanies them. We saw in chapter 3 that in Hebrew the verb "to make" is always accompanied by a statement of the purpose of the work of making. In this regard, to understand God to have made us "in" his image utterly fails to agree with the Hebrew word "make." However, if we see here an explanation of the purpose for which we are made, "in the role of our image and for an expression of our likeness," then there is perfect agreement between the verb and the preposition. The verb "to make" requires that we find here or nearby the purpose and reason for which God made us. There simply is no other adequate candidate for this

---

6. Gen. 3:15 KJV; NIV "crush."

7. Jonathan Edwards, *The Freedom of the Will* (Morgan, Pa.: Soli Deo Gloria Publications, 1996), p. 36.

function; the image and likeness provide the only viable option to express that purpose.

Thus we have five reasons to prefer the "as/for" translation instead of the "in/according to" translation.

1. "As" and "for," or more explicitly, "in the role of" and "for the purpose of," are much more synonymous and interchangeable than are "in" and "according to," which fits with 5:3's reversal of the prepositions.

2. The more traditional translations imply either a past or a present achievement and fulfillment of God's image, an implication that the rest of Scripture declines to substantiate.

3. The understanding of God's image as our role and purpose lends a forward-peering, eschatological edge to the phrase that fits more comfortably in Scripture than does the abstract anthropology inherent in more traditional interpretations of the passage.

4. Recognizing that being God's image is our role and purpose requires that our whole selves be taken up in this role and that we image God as he sees himself, not merely image an abstract concept of God. This is something that cannot be claimed even if we were to add together all of the possible understandings rendered by the "in/after" translation. All of them together would yield but a fractional image displayed on a fraction of the human individual.

5. The word "to make" requires the purpose for which we are being made to be stated, and only the reading "let us make humankind in the role of our image and for the purpose of our likeness" supplies that purpose.

Image and Likeness

At last we come to the two words that generally get the lion's share of any exposition of the passage: image (צֶלֶם, *tselem*) and likeness (דְּמוּת, *demuth*).

The word translated "image" is a relatively uncommon word, which outside of Genesis is usually used in the Old Testament to refer to material figures formed as representations, often idols. Thus images were more than mere paintings or pictures. They were three-dimensional and were meant to represent that to which they pointed, both through their appearance and through ritual (symbolic) meaning. The tumors and rats of gold formed by the Philistines were images made both to look like tumors and rats and to represent them or stand in their place.[8] Other occurrences of the word frequently are translated as "idol" and involve figures formed both to resemble and to represent gods. Once, in Psalm 73:20, a dream is also referred to as an "image."

"Likeness" (דְּמוּת, *demuth*) derives from the root דמה "to be like, resemble."[9] Its use varies but it always implies a close resemblance on some level. "They have venom *like* the venom of a serpent."[10] "King Ahaz sent to the priest Uriah a *model* of the altar."[11] "Then one in human *form* touched my lips."[12] "Listen, a noise on the mountains, *like* that of a great multitude!"[13] From these examples we can infer that the resemblance could be on any of a variety of levels. The venom spoken of resembles serpent venom not in substance but in effect; the model resembles the altar in shape though not in size or use; the noise in the mountains resembles the sound of an approaching army so as not to be distinguishable from it (it might, in fact, be the sound of an army). The similarity implied by the word דְּמוּת (*demuth*) can lie anywhere in the range from metaphoric and abstract to identity.

Why the two words? Do they refer to two different types of connections between God and us? Or should we understand the words to have a single composite meaning? The following section will attempt to build a case that while the words צֶלֶם "image" and דְּמוּת "likeness" are not equivalent, their meanings are complementary. They amplify each other rather than referring to two different things. The use of the two words reflects the fact that a full and pregnant idea is being expressed, and to use only a single word, even if it fulfilled the meaning, would leave an emotional void. The Bible is replete with this literary device of pairing words and ideas, especially in the Old Testament, and the effect is to increase the emotional impact and the urgency of the message, as well as to sharpen the focus on the subject. The singleness of the meaning is evident from the fact that the use of one of the terms independent of the other does not represent a contrast, but rather represents the whole of the meaning of

---

8. 1 Sam. 6:5, 11.
9. Wenham, *Genesis*, p. 29.
10. Ps. 58:4 NRSV.
11. 2 Kgs. 16:10 NRSV.
12. Dan. 10:16 NRSV.
13. Isa. 13:4 NIV.

both terms together. In other words, there is no reason to understand the reference in 1:27 (see also Genesis 9:6), "in the image of God he created them," to be denying that or subtracting from the statement that we are also created in God's likeness. The term "image" stands in for the whole idea that we are created for the image/likeness of God.

But before embarking on the long discussion of grammatical hermeneutics that follows, let us take note of some simple and commonsense evidence for the joint import of the two words.

In Genesis 5:3 Adam's son is said to be "in his likeness, according to his image." If we differentiate strongly between the two words in 1:26, then we will need to follow through in 5:3. Do "image" and "likeness" there also designate resemblances in the spirit and in the body between Adam and Seth, or in intellect and original purity? Such seem to be very difficult readings. Instead, the weight of the passage, being the beginning of a genealogy, is on Seth's role as Adam's successor through whom Adam's race would be perpetuated.

It has been suggested that the phrase in Genesis 5:3 represents Adam and Eve's naive surprise at the resemblance to themselves of this son: "Oh, look, Adam, he looks like you and resembles you!" This suggestion is rather farfetched, however, for Cain and Abel had already been born, yet for neither of them was the remark recorded that they were the image and likeness of Adam. Our first parents were not expecting Eve to bear a child resembling an aardvark. In fact, Seth's birth is recorded in chapter 4 with no such comment given until he is mentioned at the beginning of the genealogy. It seems to be his role in this genealogy, as the son through whom Adam would be perpetuated, and through whom the second Adam would come, that earns him this epithet. Remember that although Cain is alive at this point, he (his seed) will not be alive after the flood, by the time that Moses writes this book.

Taken with what was said regarding the prepositions above, we could say that Seth was born in the role and for the purpose of being his father's successor. As the successor he was also heir to all that was his father's. Similarly we understand concerning the inception of mankind, that we are created in the role and for the purpose of being God's image and likeness to all of creation and even to the Creator. And, like Seth, we are heirs (co-heirs with Christ) of all that is our Father's. We too are created for the purpose of following in our Father's footsteps and of bringing honor to him by living as he lives. This is our role in God's cosmic drama.

The Gloss

If the Bible were to say that Goliath was "tall and stupid," then we would understand that two different traits were being attributed to Goliath. If it then later mentioned "tall Goliath," we might remember that he is also stupid, but we would not be able to say that his stupidity is included in the fact that he is tall. King Saul was also very tall, but was not reputed to be stupid. However, when the Bible says that God is merciful, abounding in loving-kindness, we see immediately that these two are being joined together. Mercy expresses his loving-kindness and his loving-kindness calls forth his mercy. If we later read that his loving-kindness never wanes, we should bring to the new text our understanding that his loving-kindness is intertwined with his mercy, so we know that his mercy will not grow tired of being expressed toward us.

In such pairings, we sometimes refer to the second term as a gloss of the first. Thus, loving-kindness is a gloss for God's mercy. Of course, the order of the pairing will often change, so which one is considered the gloss for the other is of little importance; they are linked, not as one superior and one inferior, but as two concepts that help to fill out the expression of an idea that is overflowing with richness. Our understanding neither of mercy nor of loving-kindness ultimately does justice to God's attitude and determined stance toward us. Therefore they are paired to expand each other and to guide us to see that the author is straining to express a concept that is beyond our language. Poetic devices often point in this way to concepts that lie beyond the scope of our language and our understanding. The very tension created by the straining of the words has the effect of expanding the reach of our understanding and, ultimately, of directing our attention to the inexpressibility of the concept.

To be considered a gloss, the second must be to some extent a renaming of the first, not a mere addition to the first. The example above of Goliath being tall and stupid, then, could not be a gloss, for the statement of his stupidity in no way renames his tallness. The two terms, neither being a restatement of the other, remain distinct statements about Goliath: the one adds to the other. To function as a gloss, the second term must be nearly synonymous with the first, as in our second example.

This pairing of words functions in a way that is strikingly similar to the working of allusion in literature. Allen Pasco defines allusion as:

> The metaphorical relationship created when an alluding text evokes and uses another, independent text. Neither the reference nor the

referent, it [the allusion] consists in the image produced by the metaphoric combination that occurs in the reader's mind.[14]

Thus, there is a current text that in some way alludes, or points back, to an earlier text. But neither of these is the allusion. Rather, the two texts are integrated in the reader's mind and together produce a third text, which Pasco calls the "metaphorical text." It is that metaphorical text, the one created in the reader's mind during the integration of the earlier text into the newer text, that Pasco calls the "allusion." Therefore the most vital text, and the best one for the reader to dwell upon, is the one that exists not on any page but rather in the reader's mind.

> One should recognize that allusion is more than the external term or intertext, indeed, more than the sum of the internal and external terms. It is a *relationship* between a minimum of two terms that, through varying degrees of parallels or oppositions, creates a new entity greater than any of its constituent parts. It is this metaphoric creation or "event" that stands above the constituent texts, since it incorporates them.[15]

Likewise, the pairing of words in the form of a gloss will form a third term, which we may call a metaphorical term, which exists in the reader's mind rather than on the printed page. Nevertheless, it is this third term that constitutes the *real* and the *vital* text. A true reading will be one in which this derived term predominates in the reader's imagination, rather than a disintegrated reading of the two individual terms. Just as with allusion, "we are encouraged to rise above the elements without negating them, to put them together, and to experience the resultant image."[16]

God's mercy and his loving-kindness are very similar concepts, although they are by no means equivalent. No two synonyms are really equivalent; there is always some amount of differentiation in meaning, nuance, usage, or at least tonal quality. Even if all else could be equivalent, the sound in our ear and the feel in our mouth would still differentiate words to us. Therefore, there can be no perfect synonyms. It is in these subtle differentiations of near synonyms that the use of a gloss gains its power. While we intuitively understand from the pairing of two words that seem to denote just about the same thing the fact that they are each pointing toward the same concept, those shades of difference create a tension within us that draws us into the striving toward fuller understanding.

14. Allan H. Pasco, *Allusion: A Literary Graft* (Toronto: Univ. of Toronto Press, 1994), p. 12.
15. Ibid, pp. 13-14.
16. Ibid, p. 14.

We are thus involved in the author's struggle for expression; we too ache to find the right words. A gloss is, therefore, most potent when the intrinsic unity is at once apparent, yet the tension between the two expressions requires the greatest struggle to coalesce in our minds. If there is no sense of struggle or tension between the two terms, then the gloss will strike us as petty and impotent. As the reader enters into the author's struggle, resolution of the tension between the terms is found in the recognition of a third term, a metaphorical term, that supercedes the two explicit terms.

An author who is seeking to express a vital and vibrant concept will, then, sometimes seek a strong pairing of words and will seek to unite concepts that are too disparate for some readers to intuit that they are meant to refer to a single concept, that they are playing off of each other. When God said, "I form the light, and create darkness: I make peace, and create evil," it is easy to miss the pairing of the words "light" and "peace," and of "darkness" and "evil."[17] Until their essential unity is brought to mind, the significance of God's words and the power of the glosses remain muted.

It is plain then that the reader will sometimes miss what an author intended to be a gloss, or renaming, and will read a phrase as if the author referred to two different concepts instead of one. Indeed, the more potent a gloss the author attempts to make, the more disparity the author feels inclined to introduce between the terms, the greater likelihood that readers will miss the gloss altogether.

When we are in doubt as to whether an author intends to refer to one concept by two different names or to refer to two distinct concepts, how may we ascertain which is in fact the case? In many cases there is no "rule" to follow other than our own cautious judgment. Not all hermeneutical questions can be answered with certainty, at least not such certainty as would satisfy all readers. However, in some cases there may be one test that will yield a nearly foolproof judgment. When a pair of words is used in what might or might not be a gloss, if either of the words later stands independent of the other, in relation to the same subject, without any apparent loss of meaning compared with when the two words were used in tandem, then we can be confident that the second term was a gloss of the first.

That is a mouthful, but it is a very simple test, when an author has provided the opportunity for us to use it. The text that provides the subject for this book also provides an excellent opportunity to employ this test: "Then God said, 'Let us make man in our image, in our likeness.'"

---

17. Isa. 45:7 KJV.

The terms "image" and "likeness" are similar enough that many readers will immediately see here a double naming of one concept: something that we might express as God's "image/likeness." There is, however, sufficient differentiation that many other readers will be equally convinced that the image and the likeness are two distinct entities, quantities, or qualities. Indeed, this perceived dichotomy formed the very foundation of Augustine's and many other eminent scholars' interpretation of the passage. Among other considerations was the simple fact that such a duality allowed interpreters to deduce that God's image persisted while his likeness was destroyed.

But, let us look at verses 26 and 27 together.

> Then God said, "Let us make man in our image, in our likeness, and let them rule over the fish of the sea and the birds of the air, over the livestock, over all the earth, and over all the creatures that move along the ground."
>
> So God created man in his own image,
> in the image of God he created him;
> male and female he created them.[18]

The terms "image" and "likeness" from the first sentence must refer to either one thing or to two things. Either way, they express God's intent in creating humanity. Then we come to the first word of the next sentence: "so." "So" introduces the result of God's determination. God decided to do something, and we immediately see that God accomplished it. But what does the text tell us? It says that God created man in the role of his own image; it then reiterates that in the role of the image of God he created him. The word "likeness" is dramatically missing. Do we therefore conclude that God failed with regard to his likeness or that he changed his mind? Is it not more reasonable to understand from this word "image" all that had been expressed earlier by the pair of words, "image" and "likeness"? Indeed, beginning the sentence with the word "so" cues us to understand that this sentence follows logically from the previous one. We must understand this statement to serve the same purpose as the earlier refrains, "and it was so."

That is what was meant, in the hermeneutical rule stated earlier, by one term standing independent of the other term, but lacking none of the meaning of the pair of words working together. "Image" and "likeness" have been linked already; now either will be able to fill in for the pair when they are used in relation to the same subject, the making of humanity. The

---

18. Gen. 1:26–27 NIV.

In the Role of God's Image

one word "image" is now equivalent by itself to both itself and its gloss together. This judgment is again emphasized when God tells Noah that "in the image of God has God made man."[19] Again there is no hint that God's likeness is absent, either before or after the fall, but the one word now pulls the weight of both. Indeed, this could hardly fail to be the case if they were both pointing to the same concept from the beginning.

To sum up the argument, would anyone say that the lights in Genesis 1 were placed in the sky to perform two functions: to *preside* over the day and the night, and to *separate* light from darkness (1:18)? Or in 1:28 is God blessing humankind with three separate instructions: *be fruitful, multiply,* and *fill the earth*? These are not multiple blessings but rather parallel instructions that enhance each other and fill out the meaning and sense of the blessing. So it is with צֶלֶם (image) and דְּמוּת (likeness): they work together as one meaning. Such co-working of words is closely aligned with the most common poetical form in the Bible, commonly called Hebraic parallelism.[20] The second word, the gloss, is a restating of the first; however, it is often better not to take them in a particular order but to see them as equal co-workers, each amplifying the other. Thus there is no significant difference in Genesis 5:3 when their order is reversed and the prepositions are inverted. They still work together to express the single common and united meaning.

The significance of this fact lies not in the use of "image" by itself, but in the understanding that this separate use emphasizes that both "image" and "likeness" were used in naming the same relationship. With this understanding we avoid the dualistic approach to human nature that has been so often read into these words. Humanity as a whole and human beings considered as individuals are not seen in either the Hebrew Bible or the Christian Bible as spirits inhabiting bodies, or as intellects lashed to ethical concerns. Throughout the Bible, spirit, soul, body, mind, strength, imagination, and emotion are all interwoven to form one creature, the human. Genesis 1:26 in no way veers from the consistent anthropology found throughout the rest of Scripture.

While avoidance of error is a negative usage of the understanding, there is also a positive use that is more vital to our reading. Do you remember the meaning of the two words? An "image" is a physical representation of something that may or may not be physical; the most common use of the word is in referring to idols. The image need not, therefore, actually

---

19. Gen. 9:6 NIV.

20. Compare John Calvin, *Institutes of the Christian Religion*, ed. John T. McNeill and trans. Ford Lewis Battles (Philadelphia: Westminster Press, 1960), pp. 186-89.

bear any physical resemblance to the object, king, or god that is represented. In this we see that the word "tree" is an image in that it represents the idea of a tree, without regard to whether it actually resembles a tree. Simple resemblance does not disqualify one thing from being an image of another, but neither is resemblance necessarily implied.

"Likeness," by contrast, necessarily involves a resemblance between one thing and another, as, for instance, a dream. The all-important concept in the word "likeness" is in the actual resemblance, the seeming. If a sound seems to be the sound of a huge army marching, then it is the likeness of the sound of a marching army. No matter whether the sound actually comes from the wind, the ocean waves, a drug induced hallucination, or an invading army, the "likeness" lies in the seeming. There is no sense that the likeness stands in for the real thing; the noise does not stand in place of an army, the vision does not stand in place of the real thing, the model of an altar cannot be used in place of a real altar. A likeness of Jesus, no matter how well presented, must never be worshiped in his place.

The difference between these two words is truly pronounced. The degree of similarity is almost negligible. Both words express a connection between two objects, persons, or ideas, but the type of connection is radically different. Benjamin Franklin was an image of America in that he was the visible representation and ambassador of America in Europe; God be praised, he was not the likeness of America. A painting of Benjamin Franklin, on the other hand, is his likeness, but it would do no good to hold a conversation with that painting. It could not be sent to France as an ambassador.

This high level of dissimilarity between the object and its gloss indicates that the author (in this case, God) intends to express a concept that cannot be easily gotten to through simple word-definition language. In an attempt to overcome this obstacle, the author molded an expression that creates tension in the hearer through the extreme disparity of the two terms that are being united. This tension can only be relieved by the formation of a third term, a metaphorical term, that exceeds both the concept of an image and that of a likeness. Neither term was sufficient for his concept, although each expresses a close connection between God and humanity. God is expressing a vibrant relationship between these creatures and himself, a relationship that surpasses either word on its own.

We are his image/likeness, both at once, and more. On a Venn diagram this is the little area that lies within the space where the circle of the "image" domain and the circle of the "likeness" domain overlap. Humanity is made both to represent God, to stand in his place, and also to resemble him to such a degree that we might be mistaken for him. I did not say it; God did. I tremble to think it, but that is the force of the two words. Our role in creation is such that the line of separation, the border where God ends and humanity begins, must become blurred and obscured. Anything less would fail to rise to the level of God's image/likeness.

The fact that these two words are being used together to indicate a single concept absolutely rules out any suggestion that Adam ever realized the fulfillment of this proposition. Let me explain. Were we taking the sum of the two domains, the sum of all that is the image plus all that is the likeness of God, then that sum would be much larger than either. We are, however, not taking the sum but dealing with a weightier concept that is pointed to by the convergence of the two; we have in view only that which is properly the image and the likeness of God at the same time. This convergence renders a very much smaller set than would the sum of the two.

That which answers to the image would include God's Word, the Bible. It stands in his place in that it speaks to us for him and we are going to be judged according to our submission to it because it is his voice to us. And yet the Bible is not God nor is it easy to imagine ourselves thinking that it is. The Bible is not God's likeness. It is his representative among us; it is his self-disclosure, yet it remains only a communication to us rather than an Emmanuel. "Thy word have I hid in mine heart, that I might not sin against thee."[21] The distinction between God and his Word never gets blurred. It never rises to the level of his likeness.

Looking in the opposite direction we see that there are those who bear a likeness to God but who fail to represent him; they represent themselves, rather, as more than they are. The New Testament renders "likeness of God" into the word "godliness." While we are instructed to pursue this likeness to God in many places, we are also warned that some may display the outward appearance (μόρφωσιν, *morphōsin*) of God's likeness without admitting to being under his authority.[22] It is perfectly possible for people to seem to display God's love, God's patience, and God's compassion without being God's ambassadors.

Anyone who has seen the movie *Gandhi* will know what this means. Mohandas Gandhi gave every indication of being a very godlike person, not that he created something from nothing, but that he displayed superhuman compassion toward his fellow human creatures and expressed this

---

21. Ps. 119:11 KJV.

22. For instructions to pursue God's likeness, see 1 Tim. 2:2; 4:7-8; 6:3-11; 2 Pet. 1:6-7; 3:11. For the warning that a form of such likeness (*morphōsin*) to God is possible even in the damned, see 2 Tim. 3:5.

compassion in such altruistic ways that he truly seems to have loved others more than himself. That is truly Godlike; it exemplifies the manner in which Jesus loved his Father and gave himself over to pursue his Father's will instead of his own. He even cited Jesus' example on the cross as a part of what led him to his understanding of nonviolent resistance. So Gandhi's Godlike exhibition of suffering for others was in part an expression of what he had learned from God. Yet he insisted that Jesus' death on the cross was only a great example for us, not *the* sacrifice for us to bring us to God. We need not doubt that Mohandas Gandhi performed his works with absolute integrity, for we have Scripture's teaching that even such an exemplary person as Gandhi could indeed display much of God's character without being God's image, without living under God's authority, without being God's ambassador.

But to be both fully God's image and fully his likeness requires much more. It requires much more than Adam ever had the privilege of fulfilling during his lifetime. He was God's appointed emissary, yet he never displayed God's character to the extent required by this pairing of words. The tension inherent in unifying the pair leads us to understand that the author is seeking to describe a difficult concept. The words themselves end up not defining that concept but rather pointing at it. God's image/likeness is in fact even more elusive than that tiny area where the two circles of the Venn diagram overlap. It is more elusive and more exclusive. But exactly how exclusive must be merely pondered; it is not fully defined in this verse.

In fact, it will not be fully defined in this lifetime. But a few hints are available if we ponder the image/likeness in light of God's triune nature, his self-sacrificial love, the scraps of eschatology in Scripture, and the rest of God's workings on behalf of *adam*. A tiny portion of these hints will be considered in the second half of this book.

6

God's Self-Revelation

WHAT IS the sum of the previous five chapters' exegesis of Genesis 1:26? To what have we come in the first half of this book?

> Before the creation of Adam, God the Father invited his Son and his Spirit to join him in making a creature for the purpose of expressing and manifesting their own Trinitarian character and manner of life.

That is it. But, dear reader, you were warned in the Preface that it would all come down to that. The rest, as we said, is details. The past few chapters have sought to establish and defend this thesis. Thus far, the discussion has focused overwhelmingly on the four words that are the fountainhead of this doctrine. However, God's preoccupation with his image does not end there. There is more that can be said about God's image and more that can be learned from it. The next few chapters will consider briefly the implications of God's purpose for us in terms of systematic and biblical theology as well as seeking to fill out the concept in light of God's unveiling of his purposes for humanity throughout Scripture, but will attempt no thorough treatment of either. Before we begin, let us concisely expound the statement above as it has been seen in the preceding chapters.

The Doctrine of God's Image in Brief

Because humans were created as God's image, "human dignity comes not from any traits inside of ourselves, but from a role imposed upon us by our Creator at the time of our creation." "God did not make mankind with his image as one, or some, or all of our characteristics. God made humans expressly to *be* his image."[1]

We are the work of God. This is not to be understood as simply that we are the product of his work in the first six-day creation, but that his

---

1. Douglas P. Baker, "The Image of God: According to Their Kinds," *Reformation and Revival Journal* 12, no. 2 (Spring 2003): 101.

work continues. Furthermore, as Jesus made clear, God's creative enterprise is not the work of one person alone, but is the work of three: Father, Son, and Spirit. What these three have undertaken, we can trust will be accomplished.

Four facts should impress themselves on us regarding ourselves as being God's image:

1. We do not currently see ourselves reflecting God's image.
2. God's work continues.
3. The saints are still being made into God's image.
4. God's image is to be displayed not only in individuals, but more fully in the interrelationships between individuals, in the union of individuals. Only together can we display the image of the Trinity.

The Trinitarian work of making us into God's image is not finished. It has always been our role and our purpose, but it has never been our achievement. We were made for the purpose of displaying God's image, but we have not yet fulfilled that purpose. God's image should be understood eschatologically as the goal toward which God has been working throughout history, the fulfillment of which we can confidently anticipate. Likewise, as our teleology, as our purpose both in history and in eternity, it should be our fervent wish to finally see this fulfillment and to work toward that end; in this we have the privilege of becoming colaborers with God, for he too is working toward the manifestation of his image in us.

Because our role is set for us by God's purpose and proposed plan, it can neither fail nor falter. The fact that we do not presently look like God's image has nothing whatever to do with the validity of the statement that we currently exist to be his image. Our purpose is not dependent on our achievement.

To be God's image is to display him fully, to display the life of the Trinity. Since our role has such large scope, no proposed understanding of God's image that sees us as displaying just a tiny portion of God will do.

Ultimately, we will not only display the life of God, we will participate in it.

Now let us consider how this doctrine of God's image is integral to God's dealings with humanity. Again, this will be anything but a full systematic treatment, but it is hoped that it will be sufficient to demonstrate that such treatment is possible and worthwhile.

God's Image as Self-Revelation

When God said, "Let us make humankind in our image, according to our likeness," notice who was taking responsibility for making us in his image. God himself was. This point is very important for a couple of reasons. First, God will not fail in this proposal any more than he fails in any other proposal. Because God decided to make us to be his image, we will finally fulfill that role and become that which we were created to be.

Equally significant to the present discussion is that God is proposing to make us in his own self-image. If God is doing the making and if he says that what he is making is to be his image, the result will be a disclosure not only of God but also of God as he sees himself. Is there a difference? Does God know himself well enough to paint a thorough and accurate self-portrait? The obvious answers are "No" and "Yes." There is no difference. God's disclosure of himself will correspond just as well to God in his person (as he really is) as to God in his own eyes (as God sees himself).

Then why bother to mention it? Because historically every major stream of interpretation of what it means to be created in God's image has stumbled at this point. In light of our earlier discussion we may ask, If the creation of humankind is an act of self-disclosure on God's part, why should we not expect that God's image will encompass the whole of God and his glory? Are we afraid to look so high because we do not now see God's glory in ourselves? Where ought we to look, to ourselves or to God, in order to determine how we are to understand God's image?

Historically theologians have automatically turned from the subject, namely God, to the object, which is us.[2] They cast their gaze upon us as we now stand after the Fall rather than how we stood before the Fall, and then bring to bear upon the topic all the light that each theologian's anthropology can supply.[3] But we are not the subject or focus of this doctrine: God is. God is his own focus in this proposal to make us and he should remain our focus in interpretation.

Adam was moderately aware of who God is because he and God walked together in the garden. But where do we look to see God? We look to God's expression of himself in his Word, the Bible, and especially in

---

2. Consider God's words as they appear in the sentence: Us (subject), let make (verb), *adam* (direct object). Grammatically the subject is the doer of the verb, and in this case God is the doer of this verb. The subject of God's proposal is not "*adam*"; rather, the plural "God" is the subject.

3. For fuller treatment of how theologians' understanding of God's image has been shaped by their understanding of anthropology, see Karl Barth, *Church Dogmatics* (Edinburgh: T & T Clark, 1958), 3,1:192–94.

his incarnate Word, Jesus. God has shown himself to us as he walked in the garden, as he sat under the tree at Abram's tent, as he spoke from the burning bush, and as he conversed with Moses on Mt. Sinai. He wrestled with Jacob as a man, spoke to Elijah as a gentle whisper, and stood with the three Hebrew children in Nebuchadnezzar's fire. God has revealed himself in many places and in many ways, but his self-revelation reached its culmination in his Son who is "the reflection of God's glory and the exact imprint of God's very being."[4]

If the self-revelation that we see of God in his Word is long and complex, full of questions and impenetrable mystery, how dare we interpret his self-disclosure in and through us in a reductionist one-dimensional framework? Someone will ask how I would dare to speak of humanity in such a way, as though we were God's self-disclosure in some way equal to the Bible or to Jesus. I respond simply with the words of our text, "Let us make humankind in our image, according to our likeness." The words "image" and "likeness" encompass such a fullness of meaning as to leave no place for partial images and skewed likenesses. God has proposed an act of self-expression, a work of self-disclosure, and we are it. Our perspectives fall back inert into the dust, for "what we will be has not yet been revealed. What we do know is this: when he is revealed, we will be like him, for we will see him as he is."[5]

Continuity of God's Image

Just as it was God's word that made lights appear and his word that made fish swim and birds fly, so also it is his word that makes us his image. All people were made and remain God's image by divine decree. Note that Genesis 9:6 says as much:

> Whoever sheds the blood of a human,
>   by a human shall that person's blood be shed;
> for in his own image
>   God made humankind.[6]

Here we see that God is defending the lives of those who lived after the flood, each born and steeped in sin, on the basis that they are created in his own image. God has not ceased to consider them to be his image. There is continuity to God's image, a continuity that is not adequately

---

4. Heb. 1:3 NRSV.
5. 1 John 3:2–3 NRSV.
6. Gen. 9:6 NRSV.

taken into account by those holding a view of God's image as the original purity in which we were formed at creation. In at least one sense, that of which God spoke in Genesis 9:6, I am God's image just as Adam was.

The Lack of God's Image

At the same time it is clear that modern humanity does not represent God with any clarity, so much so that Jesus said of some, "You are from your father the devil."[7] They and we do not display God's image. So there remains another sense in which we are not God's image.

These two senses must be kept clear and distinct and both must be affirmed without allowing one to encroach on or displace the other. Yet they are linked. An undue dissimilarity must not be thrust between them.

The situation is similar to that of soteriology in which we are accustomed to saying, "I was saved," "I am saved," and "I will be saved." All three of these are true in distinct ways, and the truth of each in no way limits the truth of the others. To say that I will be saved when Jesus sits in judgment on his throne does not imply that it is not also true that I was fully and finally saved almost two thousand years ago on a cross outside of Jerusalem. Their meanings are intimately linked and inseparable; they are complementary, not at odds.

To see how we both are and are not God's image, we must understand God's image as the role into which he created us. We were created for this purpose and with this goal. The purpose of our creation was that we might be a living embodiment of his glory. His glory is our whole purpose and reason for being. Tiny things such as are discussed in other understandings of God's image grow pale in comparison. We were made to mirror God's glory to each other, to all creation, and especially to God himself. This mandate encompasses our entire person, our entire race, all aspects of our lives, all of our history, and even all of our future. And it encompasses all of God's glory.

When we ponder the sweep of our mandate, we are struck with wonder that we have been made to display his glory. That is the role for which God made us and in which God continues to see us.

At this point, an analogy from our own sphere of reference may help us to understand. When a king sends an ambassador to another kingdom, his purpose is that the ambassador will represent him well. That is the ambassador's role. If the representative misbehaves, he must answer to his own king. However, regardless of how that ambassador behaves, the way

---

7. John 8:44 NRSV.

he is treated by his hosts will be taken as if it were done to the king himself. If the ambassador is abused, that will be seen as a direct insult to the king and his kingdom. We have no difficulty imagining that an ambassador is simultaneously the representative of his king and no representation of him at all; he can live in a role without fulfilling it.

Similarly, we are sent as God's ambassadors. We will answer to him for our representation of him, and he takes as a personal affront any mistreatment of us. We are his.

We are ambassadors and representatives. God ordained this role for us, and it is not up to us either to accept or to reject it. It just is. We do not accept or reject our role as citizens, but the laws of the land are binding on us nonetheless, and breaking them subjects us to just penalties.

Sadly, we must acknowledge that we do not fulfill our role. We look more like God's enemy than like God. Therefore, it can be said that we are not God's image insofar as we do not fulfill that role. Not fulfilling our role is the essence of sin; it is falling short or missing the mark. But God, who is rich in mercy, has set himself to complete the work that he began at creation, and he will bring his work to completion.[8] This purpose is our eschatological end. We will finally be as we were created to be: the image, or mirror, of all of the glory of God.

In the years following Jesus' ascension a great mystery was revealed that had been hidden from eternal ages, "so that through the church the wisdom of God in its rich variety might now be made known."[9] Jesus, our head, had ascended and had sent his Spirit to inhabit his body, which is the church.[10] The church is not depicted in the New Testament as a group of little Christs, but as a single living and functioning body in which each follower of Christ forms a part and has a function.[11] It is now seen (as it could not have been seen before the church age) that ultimately it is only together with all the rest of Christ's body that we are being transformed into his image. God is far too great for his image to be fully realized in any one of us, even in our resurrected and perfected bodies. Though such thoughts are too great for us to comprehend, we may thank God that he is the master builder and architect who said, "I will build my church."[12]

---

8. See Col. 3:10; 2 Cor. 3:18; 1 Cor. 15:49; Phil. 1:6.
9. Eph. 3:10 NRSV.
10. See Eph. 1:22–23, 5:23.
11. See Rom. 12:4; 1 Cor. 12:12–31.
12. Matt. 16:18 NIV.

Human Glory and Satan's Hatred

Since it is the very basis and ground on which God created us, we would expect the idea of God's image to remain a significant part of our understanding of God's relationship with us. Oddly, even in such a detailed work as Calvin's *Institutes*, only about six pages (from more than 1,500 pages) have been set aside to contemplate the doctrine of God's image, and the idea is treated in passing only three or four more times throughout the entire work. In this "oversight" Calvin is typical, for rarely is the image of God brought to bear in a significant way in any theological treatise except those that have the concept itself as their focus.[13] In stark contrast, understanding God's image as our role rather than the blueprint by which we were made allows the image of God to maintain relevance throughout Scripture, theology, and life.

The facets of humanity on which most theories of God's image focus are large and immensely significant aspects of our character and lives: our physical appearance; our will to power and longing to be in control; our creativity; our capacity to reason, to anticipate, and to plan; our urge to pair off and become attached to each other in a Trinity-imitating union of plural becoming singular. But none of these individually nor all of them taken together constitute the essence of our humanity (much less are they the essence of the Godhead). They are only tools built into us as means to an end, and that end is far greater than we have ever imagined. It is that we reflect the love and mercy, the joy and fullness, in short the whole glory of our Creator—and with the real possibility of doing so. Our role is to show forth in ourselves as individuals and even more so in ourselves as a group a true picture of God's essential character. That is the glory of our creation and that is the eschatological end toward which God continues to draw his people.

God did not first create us and only later come down to begin a relationship with us. Our relationship to our Creator began earlier, when God first conceived of us, before we ever met him in the garden. We are his people and he is our God. We and God are inextricably linked, due to God's prior initiative, in a bond that precedes and surpasses all of God's earthly covenants with humankind. Even before our natures were formed, God had already bound himself to us. This free action on God's part is

---

13. Indeed, the phrase "image of God" is thrust into many arguments, both theological and social, but typically with no elaboration or explanation of the term, and it is generally difficult to determine exactly what the phrase is meant to convey and what content it carries.

the deeper magic that goes back even before the dawn of time.[14] All that we find in our natures—our bodies, emotions, reasoning, relationships, responsibilities, and moral conscience—is given us in service of our prior and overarching purpose of mirroring God.

Why did God not annihilate us when we rebelled? Did he not think that we deserved it? Was he bound by any covenants made with us? Not yet. But he was bound by something that would become the progenitor of all of the covenants. It was his own glory. As his image we were made to be the reflection of his glory. God put his own glory on the line in making us, because we were to represent not ourselves but him. To have annihilated us would have allowed our defamation to be an unanswered slander against his character. But God is patient and longsuffering; in his love he had determined beforehand to build us slowly into the image for which we were created. For his own glory's sake he would neither abandon us in our vileness nor destroy us. To this end he enacted covenants and began to draw a people aside and to move them step by step toward the fulfillment of the eschatological purpose for which humanity had been created.

What motivated Satan to attack us with special malevolence, out of all of the creatures God had created? His hatred of us is treated as a foregone conclusion in the opening chapters of Genesis. We never had to do anything to provoke him. Why? To this question the attribute and physical likeness theories offer no suggestions. He just hated us. Purity theory offers a reasonable answer: that Satan hated our purity and contrived to spoil it as his own had been spoiled, thus making us resemble himself. Purity theorists explain that Satan diverted us from being God's image to become a reflection of his own perverted image, and only in Christ do we gain back that which we lost. Two major problems in purity theory will be dealt with soon, but it does offer a possible answer to the question of why Satan hated us and what he wanted to accomplish in attacking us.

But Satan's hatred for humankind goes deeper than just wanting company in his miserable state. He saw that we were made as divine representatives, and his hatred of God drove him to seek to abolish the extension of God's authority from the earth. What would it have meant to Satan to see God's ambassadors clearly displaying his glory in millions and billions of people united in love to God and each other around the world? Could anything have been worse for him? He had rebelled and been cast out of God's presence. Was he now going to be pursued to the ends of the universe by God's ambassadors? So Satan desired, second only

---

14. C. S. Lewis, *The Lion, the Witch, and the Wardrobe* (New York: HarperCollins, 1978), p. 163.

to the death of God himself, to destroy those whom God was sending out as his representatives. His attack on us was a circuitous attack on the one who had sent us. The attack was circuitous, but the affront was direct. Just as the mob in Baghdad acted out their enmity against Saddam Hussein by attacking his statue (image), so Satan did to us that which he desires to do to God.

7

The Trinity

IF OUR role in the universe and beyond is to imitate God and to live our corporate life and our individual lives as the Trinity live their life and their lives, then we must ask a few questions about God. Who is he? Who are they? How do they live?[1] What is the nature of the Godhead? What exactly makes three into one? What does it mean to be the image of the Trinity? Are we expected to imitate even their unity and become one with other people?

Trinity

In chapter 4 we looked briefly at the nature of the Trinity, and we saw that no priority can be given to the individuality of the three persons of the Godhead, or to the unity in which they dwell. Each aspect is absolute and unequivocal.

But what is it that unites them? And what does their unity look like? Can we even know the answers to such questions?

The Father, the Son, and the Holy Spirit are co-eternal, of one substance, and of equal glory. These truths we have heard from theologians for many years. We do not need at present to re-walk that well trodden path. Let us rather focus on the relationship between the three persons.

Contrary to much of modernity, Cornelius Van Til taught that Christians actually "do assert that God, that is, the whole Godhead, is one person."[2] Although that had been the only orthodox teaching for many

---

1. While the idea of speaking of God's "life" is awkward, there is no other word in English that would adequately fill the spot. We must guard against the tendency to think of God as existing, as if he were a rock that simply sits and never changes. Ultimately, God is unchanging, but he is not immovable nor is he inactive. He is the God who acts. From the first line of the Bible we see God neither as a fixed point of reference nor as an abstract force or idea, but as an active person. In our thinking about God we often settle for a perspective so limited that the word "life" seems too big for God, but in reality our understanding of life is far too small to describe God's existence/life/relationships.

2. Cornelius Van Til, *An Introduction to Systematic Theology* (Philipsburg, N.J.:

hundreds of years, the century preceding Van Til had been so thoroughly dominated by liberal, evolutionary, and progressive theologians that by Van Til's time his words sounded like heresy. For the time being, Kant had won and the doctrine of the Trinity had been replaced with a teaching that seemed to fit better with the supreme test of the times: comprehensibility. The biblical and historic doctrine of the Trinity was weighed in the balance and found lacking.

The word itself, however, was too ingrained in the fabric of Christian speech to be tossed aside along with the concept. This is unfortunate because it would be much easier to reclaim the concept that rightly belongs to the word if the word itself had not in the meantime become associated with other concepts that are both similar enough to be confusing, yet divergent enough in meaning to be absolutely separate teachings.

Theoretical models began to circulate that sought to smooth over the affront to human reason posed by incomprehensibility. Instead of three and one persons in the Godhead, we began to hear that the Godhead "is like the relationships of water, which whether it is ice, liquid, or steam, remains water. Just so, it was said, whether God is the Father, the Son, or the Spirit, he is still God. Or the Trinity was modeled after a man, who could be a father to his children, a husband to his wife, and a son to his parents, yet will still be the same man in all of these relationships. Such analogies are offensive to our sense of proportion, if not downright blasphemous as attempts to cram the King of the Universe into the tiny bottle of our understandings. Such a manageable definition of God yields him up to us without the need of fear, trembling, awe, or wonder."[3] It was in opposition to this trend that Van Til insisted that Christians, in fact, "do assert that God, that is, the whole Godhead, is one person."

Van Til insisted that not only is God one person while at the same time being three persons, but also that these two facts must be seen with equal ultimacy. Neither the fact of God's being one person nor the fact that Jesus is one person and the Father is one person and the Spirit is one person, which makes three persons, could be allowed to take precedence in our minds or our theology. God is one person absolutely. God is three persons absolutely. Neither absolute may become subservient to the other.

Presbyterian and Reformed, 1978), p. 229; quoted in Ralph A. Smith, *Paradox and Truth* (Moscow, Idaho: Canon Press, 2002), p. 41.

3. The quoted sentences and the following paragraphs draw on my review of *Eternal Covenant* and *Paradox and Truth*, both by Ralph A. Smith, in *Christianity and Society* 14, no. 2 (April 2004): 29–30.

For those who accepted his reasoning, Van Til's work restored the mystery to the eternal mutual indwelling of God, but how then were we to think of the three persons and of their relationships with each other? True, it is a mystery, but is it a mystery into which we can peer through the light of those writings that are "profitable for *doctrine*, for reproof, for correction, for instruction in righteousness"?[4] How do the Scriptures enlighten our understanding of this great mystery of the Godhead?

Aligning himself with Van Til's understanding of the equal ultimacy both of God's unity and of diversity within the Godhead, Ralph Smith has turned to the covenantal framework in which Abraham Kuyper had earlier expounded the concept of the Trinity.

> We then confess that in the one personality of the divine Essence there consists a three-personal distinction, which has in the covenant relation its unity and an inseparable tie. God Himself is, according to this conception, not only of every covenant, but of the covenant idea as such the living and eternal foundation; and the essential unity [of the Godhead] has in the covenant relation its conscious expression.[5]

> In the covenant relation Father, Son, and Holy Spirit aim together and each for Himself at the triumph over sin, that is, at the triumph over all that which places itself over against God as anti-God. The ground of this will in God is found in the original covenant relation in the divine Essence.[6]

As Smith has developed Kuyper's doctrine, this covenant relationship between the Father, the Son, and the Holy Spirit is seen as far more than a mere agreement between equals. It is not simply a matter of division of labor in which one decrees and another effects that decree. This intra-Trinitarian covenant precedes, at least logically, the covenant of salvation in which the three persons undertook the elevation of humanity. It is essentially a covenant of love, and that is the name applied to it by Smith. In both Kuyper and Smith, covenant is seen as the defining characteristic of the Godhead.

Smith proceeds to combine Van Til's and Kuyper's contributions, and the doctrine of the Trinity becomes really breathtaking. Being essen-

---

4. 2 Tim. 3:16 KJV.

5. Abraham Kuyper, "Dictaten Dogmatiek," trans. in Herman Hoeksema, *Reformed Dogmatics* (Grand Rapids: Reformed Free Publishing Association, 1966), p. 295; quoted in Smith, *Paradox and Truth*, p. 74.

6. Ibid., p. 78.

tial to the character of the Godhead, covenant is essential to each of the persons, for each is coterminous with the whole Godhead. Therefore, it is meaningless to conceive of the Father as existing without the Son and the Spirit, for the Father's covenant relationship with the Son and the Spirit is essential to who the Father is. Without that relationship he would not be who he is; in fact, he would not be. The Godhead as individuals require the intra-Trinitarian covenant in order to be who they are, just as much as the Godhead as a unity requires that covenant. Here again we see the equal ultimacy—as stressed by Van Til—of the unity and the trinity of God coming to the fore. While we can conceive of the Father without simultaneously conceiving of the Son, we cannot conceive of the Father without the Son.

This intra-Trinitarian covenant consists mainly in the loving mutuality with which each indwells both of the others and is indwelt by them, such that Jesus could say without blushing, "Anyone who has seen me has seen the Father."[7] In this indwelling, they love and probe each other, knowing one another to the superlative degree. And yet they are to be distinguished as individuals, each loving the others before himself and living in a family communion. While the Holy Spirit is not less than the whole Godhead, neither does he dwell apart from the whole Godhead but is perfectly and unchangingly indwelt by each of the other members of the Godhead. The same could also be said of the Father and the Son.

The members of the Trinity are not to be separated, but neither is one member to be subsumed under or collapsed into either of the others. R. C. Sproul has observed that we can distinguish between the body and the soul, but we cannot separate them, for once we separate them we have killed the person. In the same way, we can distinguish between the three persons, but we cannot separate them, for they dwell necessarily together and are covenantally wrapped up in each other's existence.

To conceive of the Father as dwelling without the Son and the Spirit is impossible, for who is the Father but the lover of the Son and the Spirit? Without them, neither is he. This same is true of each, for they subsist only in a deep covenanted communion. Without that covenant, not only are they not as we find them, but in fact they are not. Period.

This intra-Trinitarian covenant is the root from which all of the God/human covenants grow. God makes covenants with us because he is a covenant God internally and ontologically.

---

7. John 14:9 NIV.

> Covenant expresses the goal of all creation because man, God's representative and image, is destined to become covenantally one with God, sharing in the fellowship of love that is the life of the Trinity from all eternity. That final covenant conclusion is the realization of the goal of creation. The means to bring about covenantal union between God and man were also of necessity covenantal.[8]

Therefore, this internal covenant of love clarifies why God, who dwelt in eternal felicity, would desire to create humanity at all, even such humanity as we have proved to be. We provide opportunity for each person of the Trinity to fulfill his deepest longing, which is to know the others ever more deeply and to see the others exalted more highly than they already are. They work and strain to set each other higher and to show forth and draw praise to all that they have loved in each other from eternity past.

Indwelling

It is possible to use words so often that we lose sight of the fact that we have no idea what they mean. They become potholes in the highway of ideas, and though we drive over them daily without notice, eventually they can throw us out of alignment, and our steering becomes faulty. Such, I fear, may be the case with the familiar word "indwelling."

What does it mean for Jesus to say, "Thou, Father, art in me, and I in thee," or "I in them, and thou in me, that they may be made perfect in one"?[9] Such thoughts are too often passed over lightly, but what Jesus is saying has vast implications. He says that this indwelling will make us "perfect in one" just as it also makes him and his father "perfect in one." That phrase is rendered "complete unity" in the NIV, "perfected in unity" in the NASB, and "completely one" in the NRSV. Take your pick: they all describe what Jesus is going to the cross to do: "that in Himself He might make [Jews and Gentiles] into one new man."[10] He will accomplish this unity on the cross, but it will be realized by our indwelling one another.

Indwelling is the reason Christ went to the cross: to bring us as a mutually indwelling body into this mutually indwelling relationship that he shares with his Father. Indwelling filled his thoughts in his final moment alone in prayer with his Father before being sold by a friend, abandoned by his followers, murdered by strangers, and forsaken by his Father and his God. Jesus' passionate attention circles around these twin ideas of union

---

8. Ralph A. Smith, *Eternal Covenant* (Moscow, Idaho: Canon Press, 2003), p. 59.
9. John 17:21, 23 KJV.
10. Eph. 2:15 NASB.

and indwelling. Yet when we wish to understand indwelling, theologians are not much help, for unfortunately "indwelling" (*perichorisis*) is one of the least rigorously defined words in theological discussion. Like magnetism, indwelling is better described than defined; many good words can never be satisfactorily defined.

Help from a Philosopher

Although not a theologian, the chemist and philosopher Michael Polanyi described the act of indwelling more clearly than any theologian I have read. His descriptions took many forms and covered a variety of human actions and perceptions. For instance, Polanyi described a blind man using a stick to "see" in front of himself as he walks. The stick bumps over the ground in front of the blind man, causing vibrations in the stick to be transferred to his hand. If the man feels the vibrations *as* vibrations in his hand, then he is little helped by the stick. Rather, it is when he is able to no longer feel them as vibrations *at his hand* but as variation *at the end of the stick* that he begins to "see" through the stick and can walk along with confidence. When he no longer feels that it is a stick in his hand but that it is an extension of himself, he has taken the stick into himself as a part of himself and he has put himself into it. He does not think of himself as coming along behind the stick, but the stick seems to be the blind man himself, feeling his way. He has begun to indwell the stick. Polanyi explains the process:

> Anyone using a probe for the first time will feel its impact against his fingers and palm. But as we learn to use a probe, or to use a stick for feeling our way, our awareness of its impact on our hand is transformed into a sense of its point touching the objects we are exploring. This is how an interpretive effort transposes meaningless feelings into meaningful ones, and places these at some distance from the original feeling. We become aware of the feelings in our hand in terms of their meaning located at the tip of the probe or stick to which we are attending.[11]

By indwelling the stick, the blind man has become less aware of the stick and more aware through the stick of the terrain at the end of the stick. As he has come to "know" the stick intimately, he has come to see the world through the stick. It is this focusing on one thing through something else that Polanyi is calling indwelling. We dwell in that which

---

11. Michael Polanyi, *The Tacit Dimension* (New York: Anchor Books, 1967), pp. 12–13.

is nearer to us in order to focus on that which is farther away; that is, we dwell in the stick to "see" the path ahead.

Similarly, Polanyi described the act of reading as an act of indwelling. To read, we must look not so much at the letters on a page, but through them to the meaning. We must first know, accept, and agree with the basic method of the written word, and then give ourselves into this written word. One obviously cannot read until one understands that the ink on the page represents a meaning. Likewise, the skilled reader will place herself into the letters such that she is not aware of the letters themselves but rather of the meaning to which they point. As you read this paragraph, you do not ponder the letters themselves, but rather the concepts that are buried behind the letters. The degree to which one consciously sees the letters and contemplates them, is the degree to which one is not dwelling in them but is remaining aloof from them and is thus inhibited from focusing on the meaning of the words. It is only by our indwelling the words on the page that they are rendered meaningful or useful to us.

> We meet with another indication of the wide functions of indwelling when we find acceptance to moral teachings described as their *interiorization*.[12]

By interiorizing a moral teaching, letting it live in us and we ourselves living in it, we begin to see not only the teaching itself, but also everything outside of it through the lens of that moral teaching. A person may preach on the Sermon on the Mount for months without ever applying the teachings to his own life. He is clearly keeping these teachings outside of himself and is unwilling to trust himself to them, unwilling to place himself in them to live and to dwell. It requires an act of faith, of trust, to place oneself inside of anything to live and see and act through it. To dwell within anything is an act of surrender. This is easy to see in the present example of living within a moral teaching, but it is likewise true in any other act of indwelling; to read one must be willing to surrender awareness of the immediate sense perception (the sensation of seeing the words on the page) and dwell within the art of writing so as to see beyond the symbols to the meaning.

When we recognize a face we do not separate the components that make up that face but we see the face as a whole. It is remarkable that we can instantly recognize a person whom we have met but once, even if at that time they smiled and on our second meeting they are scowling. We do not need to analyze their features to make sure of ourselves: four inches

---

12. Ibid., p. 17.

from widow's peak to nose tip, three millimeter thick earlobes, left nostril slightly larger than the right. In fact we will probably not consciously notice any of these things, yet we know at a glance that it is the same person. In doing so, we "see" and comprehend the face as a whole not by seeing the individual characteristics that set that face apart from all others, but rather by indwelling them and seeing through them to the person. And, seeing the person, we do not say, "Look, there is Perry's face," but rather we say, "Look, there is Perry." We have dwelt in the visual "clues" of the face and through them seen a person.

Similarly, one is able to indwell a person just as one indwells a stick or a set of marks on a page. The process, as Polanyi describes it, is more complex but not fundamentally different. One of the simpler examples has to do with apprenticeship.

A master craftsman does work that cannot be reduced to the written word. There is no book that can teach a pupil's fingers to feel the difference between a piece of wood that can be made into a high quality violin and an identical piece that will yield only a good violin.[13] But the master craftsman knows; he can feel and see and sense the outcome that is possible from a certain piece of wood without even knowing exactly how he knows. He cannot tell, but he can show. The apprentice therefore simultaneously studies the piece of wood itself and also the master craftsman as he handles the wood. The apprentice will watch the craftsman's fingers as they move over the wood, listen to his voice as he mumbles to himself, see his face as he considers, and know the moment when the master comes to a conclusion about the wood. Over time, through close observation and mimicry of the master, the apprentice absorbs the master's connoisseurship and comes to think the master's thoughts along with him, all the while not being able to pin down exactly what set of criteria either of them is using to select the right wood for a violin. Thus, the apprentice comes to indwell the master, not only while watching him at work, but also whenever the apprentice selects wood in the future. In years to come, the apprentice may also train apprentices, who will in turn indwell him and, thereby, unknowingly indwell his master simultaneously.

Admittedly, it is a leap to move from an epistemology focused on human knowledge to one focused on God's knowledge. And yet if we tentatively carry over Polanyi's picture of indwelling we will come, I think, to more of an understanding of the relationship between the three persons of

---

13. These "craftsman" examples are based on examples in *Tacit Knowing, Truthful Knowing: The Life and Thought of Michael Polanyi* (Charlottesville, Va.: Mars Hill Audio, 1999).

the Trinity than is rendered by either ignoring the question (the usual approach, even in theological texts) or by proposing a purely mystical union. If, having tentatively applied Polanyi's epistemology to the Godhead, we find that the resulting understanding of the Godhead sheds light on the Scripture and produces results that are consistent with both the broad flow of Scripture and the particular teachings of it, then we may trust that his epistemology has provided a useful and safe hermeneutic. If not, if applying Polanyi's explanation of indwelling to the Godhead renders an understanding of God that is in conflict at any point with the inspired word, then we must reject it, at least in reference to the Trinity.

One caveat: just as much as I am convinced that Polanyi's epistemology can help us understand the union of the Trinity, I am also convinced that this is only a very partial understanding and that there is much more to be said on this subject. Even more certain is the fact that there is much more that cannot be said but must remain forever hidden in unapproachable light. What follows must not be taken as my statement on "how the Trinity works," although I do believe that it is accurate and helpful as far as it goes.

Perichoresis in Light of Polanyian Epistemology

What then does it mean for the Father to indwell the Son, and vice versa? And what does it mean to say that we are "in Christ"? How do we "become one" as Jesus and his Father are one? Can Michael Polanyi's description of indwelling help us to understand Jesus' prayer?

> My prayer is not for them alone. I pray also for those who will believe in me through their message, that all of them may be one, Father, just as you are in me and I am in you. May they also be in us so that the world may believe that you have sent me. I have given them the glory that you gave me, that they may be one as we are one: I in them and you in me. May they be brought to complete unity to let the world know that you sent me and have loved them even as you have loved me.[14]

In his high priestly prayer Jesus said, "You are in me and I am in you." For Jesus to dwell in his Father would mean that he looks at all else *through* his Father, that he determines his own priorities by judging *through* his Father. Just as the blind man "sees" through dwelling in the end of his stick, so Jesus sees the universe, humankind, and even himself by dwelling

---

14. John 17:20–23 NIV.

in his Father. Jesus attends to us through his Father in a way that resembles the blind man attending to the sidewalk through his stick, and in the process he gives himself into his Father in love and trust just as the blind man trusts himself into the care of the stick to guide him accurately.

Just as the blind man will not go out without his stick (which he indwells) by which to see his way, so Jesus does nothing apart from indwelling and being indwelt by his Father. Indeed, he said as much: "The Son can do nothing by himself; he can do only what he sees his Father doing, because whatever the Father does the Son also does." And, "By myself I can do nothing; I judge only as I hear, and my judgment is just, for I seek not to please myself but him who sent me."[15] Jesus only acts as he sees his Father acting; both his understanding and his actions are filtered through his Father.

So the Son watches his Father's face, as it were, and loves what he sees his Father loving and hates what he sees his Father hating. He applies himself to being his Father's Son, to following in his Father's footsteps; he is an apprentice. In this he does not necessarily ask of his Father all the details of how and when their work will be finished, but simply says, "I delight to do thy will, O my God."[16] As a son works with his father (or an apprentice with his master), seeking to match his work, his energy, and his will to his father's, so works Jesus with his Father. It is his delight to live as his Father's apprentice and Son, seeking always to please his Father, to be his Father's delight, and to honor and glorify his Father by being like him. In short, everything Jesus is, everything he does, everything he plans, and everything he suffers begins and ends in his focus on his Father. He lives in and through his Father. In this way, he indwells him utterly. In so doing, he has necessarily brought his Father into himself as his own center, so that while he dwells in his Father, his Father also dwells in him.

Meanwhile, God the Father's stance toward his Son might be better pictured by analogy with a mother's indwelling of her baby. A mother does not typically look at her newborn and seek to see the world through the baby's eyes, through the baby's understanding. She does not try to match her loves to the baby's loves nor her emotions to those of the child. But still, in her every thought and desire she considers not her own needs but those of the little life that depends on her.

Does she vacuum the carpet twice a day? It is not because she expects that to increase her own comfort, but because she is compelled by protective urges to make the child's environment free of any danger, which includes

---

15. John 5:19, 30 NIV.
16. Ps. 40:8 KJV.

even the minutest speck of dust. Does she wash her hands until they are chapped and raw? It is so that no unclean thing will touch her beloved. Does she suddenly find that her voice breaks into song, even when the radio is not on? She is soothing the child, singing for the little one's comfort. Love compels her to change all of her wonted habits, not because she must, but because she may. The most bashful, modest woman will suddenly surprise her friends by nursing her child when hungry, even in public, disregarding the shame that previously would have prohibited her.

She is not herself, in the sense that she is not her prior self. She is now living, seeing, thinking, feeling, and planning through her child. She is the same little girl who once laughed on her father's knee, but now she is that girl in a new relationship, one in which she lives no longer in and through her parent, but her offspring. The mother indwells her newborn, takes that newborn to her heart, and is herself indwelt. In reality, she is now more herself than ever she could have been before. She is more herself, because she is now more imitative of God the Father's indwelling love of his Son.

Like the human mother, God the Father loves his Son, he cares for his Son, he makes plans through which to exalt him, to please him, to express his own love for him. Like the human mother, God the Father dwells in his Child, not by seeking to match his own desires to those of the Son (the manner in which the Son indwells his Father), but by matching his desires to needs of the Son, by setting aside every thought of himself as he seeks only the blessing of his Son.

In this way, the Father indwells his Son, molding his own ideas and passions around what he perceives to be fit for the building up of his beloved. As a consequence, the Son is brought into his Father's center, so that he indwells his Father. Thus, the Father dwells within his Son both through the Son's love and through the Father's love. The converse is also true: the Son dwells in the Father both through his own love for his Father and through his Father's love of him. They each work and live to draw and through drawing the other one into himself.

The relationship is yet more complex. While Jesus finds all joy in knowing his Father and working alongside of him, the purpose of all his work is not simply to accomplish the work but also to know his Father more and to share even more in his work. To this end, Jesus and his Spirit cooperate to discover his secret depths, for "the Spirit searches all things, even the deep things of God. For who among men knows the thoughts of a man except the man's spirit within him? In the same way no one knows

The Trinity

the thoughts of God except the Spirit of God."[17] Jesus and his Spirit are co-workers in this great work of getting to know the Father.

It might be imagined that the Son and the Spirit already know the Father; they have been together for eternity and surely know each other inside and out. Granted. But we surely do not think that even eternity is time enough for the Spirit to have finished searching the depths of the Father's heart. If Paul was still able to use the present tense for the Spirit's work of searching the Father's heart, after an eternity in which to search, then surely no more than eternity has passed by now; the Spirit continues searching. He will remain busy for eternity, plumbing the depths of the mind and heart of the Father. The fact that this work cannot be finished is certainly not due to the Father's having put up obstacles to block his Spirit's progress. Just as he shows all his work to his Son, so also he opens his heart to the searching of his Spirit. Rather, the heart of the Father is unfathomable because it is infinite in depth, breadth, grandeur, and intricacy.

Jesus knows his Father through working alongside him much as a son or an apprentice gets to know his master through working beside him; the Spirit knows the Father through searching him directly, perhaps in some way analogous to getting to know a person through conversation, through intimate time spent together. Jesus and his Spirit, although working in different ways, each pursue the same goal; they each seek fuller knowledge of the Father.

But they do not seek this intimate knowledge as competitors for the Father's attention. Rather, they are collaborators working together. Jesus promised that his Spirit would lead the disciples into all truth; the Spirit must have been eternally accustomed to leading others deeper into truth, for in him there is no shadow of turning. The Spirit, like the Father, says, "I the LORD do not change."[18] If he was sent to the disciples to lead them into all truth, to guide them into fuller understanding, then that had eternally been his love and his habit. And the Jesus who told his disciples, "I have called you friends, for everything that I learned from my Father I have made known to you," would not hide from his beloved Spirit anything that he learned from his Father.[19] Therefore, we can call them collaborators; indeed, they might be the model for marriage, laboring together eternally in covenant love.

17. I Cor. 2:10–11 NIV.
18. Mal. 3:6 NIV.
19. John 15:15 NIV.

Absolute unity results from such absolute indwelling. Jesus "can do nothing by himself; he can do only what he sees his Father doing, because whatever the Father does the Son also does."[20] In every action of Jesus we see his Father. In his every thought his Father is present. It is in imitation of Jesus that we are "in humility [to] consider others better than [ourselves]. Each of [us] should look not only to [our] own interests, but also to the interests of others."[21] This is how Jesus honors his Father; this is how he adores his Spirit. This is the indwelling that will make us one as they are one.

This Trinitarian indwelling can be called "love," for only love selflessly gives itself away for the building up of another. It can be called "honor," for it searches out ways to honor the beloved. It can be called "faith," for each one trusts himself into the care of the others. It can be called "faithfulness," for never will it pull back from the work to which it has put its hand. It can be called "work" or "service," for they are not lax in pursuit of the good of their beloved. It can be called "humility," for they each deny themselves daily as their attention is focused outward into each other. Trinitarian indwelling is open, honest, forthright, longsuffering, eager, patient, and modest. It is eternal. It is eternally growing and deepening. It need never fear, but in fact drives out fear. It is full of joy and delight. Trinitarian indwelling is covenant love and faithfulness.

Trinitarian indwelling is the root of every commandment. Are we to love our neighbor? Are we to honor our parents? Are we to keep our oaths even when keeping them seems to be to our disadvantage? Are we to pursue justice, love mercy, exult in the right, and keep no record of wrongs? Then these are ways in which we are to imitate the Trinitarian indwelling. These, if fully followed, would make us one just as God is one.

A man asked where life is to be found. Jesus pointed him to the law.

> "What is written in the Law?" [Jesus] replied. "How do you read it?"
> He answered: "'Love the Lord your God with all your heart and with all your soul and with all your strength and with all your mind'; and, 'Love your neighbor as yourself.'"
> "You have answered correctly," Jesus replied. "Do this and you will live."[22]

Jesus' words are not sarcasm; he is not just saying, "You cannot do it but must put your trust in me to do it for you." He said, "Do this and you

---

20. John 5:19 NIV; cf. John 5:30, 15:5.
21. Phil. 2:3–4 NIV.
22. Luke 10:26–28 NIV.

The Trinity

will live," and he meant it. To keep these two commandments would be to join in the Trinitarian indwelling of the Godhead and to reproduce it in the community of *adam*. This is life. Moses had said, "Take to heart all the words I have solemnly declared to you this day, so that you may command your children to obey carefully all the words of this law. They are not just idle words for you—*they are your life*."[23] Moses was not being sarcastic either. Keeping the law is imitation of the indwelling of the Trinity; imitation of the Trinity leads toward becoming God's image; being God's image is life.

The fulfillment of God's image is when we enter into the Trinitarian indwelling (keep the greatest commandment) and reproduce it among ourselves (keep the second, which is like the first). This is our eternal purpose; to do this is life. Some have even now entered into life.

And Jesus is life. Apart from him there is no life. We do not enter into life by keeping the two commandments or the Ten Commandments or the Levitical law or the Law, the Prophets, and the Writings. We enter life through Jesus. But that life is distilled for us in the two, expanded in the ten, and interpreted with sermons, examples, and exhortations in the Law, the Prophets, and the Writings. The law does not impart life; it is life. God's law is the expression of his own character, of the relationship that unites the Trinity; God's law is a blueprint for the expression of his image.

God, having set himself to the task of making a creature that dwells in a community resembling the community of the Trinity, will not rest until he has accomplished all that he has said. Therefore, God's law is not only our judge and condemner, but in Jesus it is also our hope and our certain future. The law is not dead to us nor we to it. It is still sweeter than honey sucked from the comb.[24] God's law is eternal; it is the future blessing in which we will dwell eternally.

Those four words that God spoke, נַעֲשֶׂה אָדָם בְּצַלְמֵנוּ כִּדְמוּתֵנוּ, "Let us make *adam* for our image and to be our likeness," are the super-concentrated expression of our creation (hence the creation of the rest of the universe), our purpose and role, God's perfect law, sin and righteousness, God's labors on our behalf, the meaning of history, Jesus' life, death, and resurrection, and God's plan for his saints. Where else do so few words contain so much?

Although we began by using a human theory of indwelling to help us probe, however feebly, into the life of the Trinity, we see that, in fact,

---

23. Deut. 32:46–47 NIV; italics added.
24. See Ps. 19:10.

the Trinity offers to us the model for how we may live in unity without diminishing our individuality. Having ruminated for a little while on the analogy from the human to the Trinitarian, ultimately we must turn around and apply the lifestyle of the Trinity to our own lives as individuals and to our corporate life.

The ultimate fulfillment of our role in creation will be to fully manifest such mutual indwelling among ourselves that we will be united as one. When we as a community of saints are able to say, "I, the *adam* you made, am one," with as much integrity as it is said by Yahweh, then and only then will we be living in fulfillment of the purpose for which we have been made.

8

Covenant

Humanity was made to express within itself the same mode of life that the Trinity enjoys. We have defined that life as a life in covenanted unity, which covenant already binds us together, but we do not yet see the covenant fulfilled. At present, we all live as covenant breakers.

The intrinsic unity of humankind, which we first see implied by God before our creation, was established physically and covenantally in the creation of Eve. After that covenant (as well as the covenant of obedience between us and God) had been broken and our parents expelled from Eden, those original covenants were, in a sense, melded and brought to a greater fulfillment in the cross of Christ. That new covenant in Jesus' blood not only guaranteed with utmost certainty the re-establishment and future fulfillment of the union covenant of Eve, but it also established a far greater union of humanity with our Creator.

While this "new" covenant was new in that it had not been seen on earth prior to its inauguration through the sacrifice of Jesus, it was not new cosmically. The massive scope of the new covenant "was in accordance with the eternal purpose that he has carried out in Christ Jesus our Lord."[1] God had made it his "eternal purpose" to unite humankind into a single bride for his beloved Son and to bind them to him eternally in the covenant of marriage.

Covenant

The term "covenant" has been defined in many ways through the ages, but one of the most concise definitions that does justice to the word as it is used in Scripture is that offered by O. Palmer Robertson, who wrote that "a covenant is a bond in blood, or a bond of life and death, sovereignly administered."[2]

---

1. Eph. 3:11 NRSV. For the full context (united to Christ, united to others through Christ, and so forth), see 2:11–3:19.
2. O. Palmer Robertson, *The Christ of the Covenants* (Philipsburg, N.J.: Presbyterian

There are three main components that Robertson finds integral to covenants: a bond, blood or lifeblood, and sovereign administration. To help clarify the importance of these three, let us consider them in the context of the covenant between Laban and Jacob.

When Jacob fled from the home of his father-in-law, he left with bad blood between them. Jacob felt that he had been mistreated by his father-in-law and had been cheated repeatedly on his wages and lied to concerning Laban's daughter, Rachel. At the same time, Laban and his sons had begun resenting Jacob, thinking that he was robbing them of their flocks while shepherding their sheep. So when the disappearance of Jacob and his wives, their children, servants, and flocks, not to mention their household idols, was discovered, Laban was furious. He gathered a small army of sons and servants, pursued Jacob's caravan, and overtook it. Heated words were exchanged, and Laban searched for his idols, but did not find them. When the search was ended, it was Jacob's turn to explode with rage.

> Although you have felt about through all my goods, what have you found of all your household goods? Set it here before my kinsfolk and your kinsfolk, so that they may decide between us two.[3]

Jacob wanted justice to be decided; he wanted the evidence laid out, if there was any. But what would have been gained? Laban would have gone home feeling wronged; Jacob would have continued on his way bearing his fear and anger toward his father-in-law into his homeland. Each would have lived in perpetual fear of retribution from the other, and each would have felt himself justified in pursuing such retribution. Therefore, Laban proposed,

> "Come now, let us make a covenant, you and I; and let it be a witness between you and me." So Jacob took a stone, and set it up as a pillar. And Jacob said to his kinsfolk, "Gather stones," and they took stones, and made a heap; and they ate there by the heap. Laban called it Jegar-sahadutha: but Jacob called it Galeed. Laban said, "This heap is a witness between you and me today." Therefore he called it Galeed, and the pillar Mizpah, for he said, "The LORD watch between you and me, when we are absent one from the other. If you ill-treat my daughters, or if you take wives in addition to my daughters, though no one else is with us, remember that God is witness between you and me."

---

and Reformed, 1980), p. 4.

3. Gen. 31:37 NRSV.

Covenant

> Then Laban said to Jacob, "See this heap and see the pillar, which I have set between you and me. This heap is a witness, and the pillar is a witness, that I will not pass beyond this heap to you, and you will not pass beyond this heap and this pillar to me, for harm. May the God of Abraham and the God of Nahor"—the God of their father—"judge between us." So Jacob swore by the Fear of his father Isaac, and Jacob offered a sacrifice on the height and called his kinsfolk to eat bread; and they ate bread and tarried all night in the hill country.[4]

Here we see that a covenant was created in which Jacob and Laban became bound to honor the boundary marker between their lands, and to pass it neither to steal from the other nor to attack the other. And Jacob was further bound by this covenant to take no further wives, besides the two daughters of Laban who were already married to him, and to treat them gently. This covenant established a new relationship between the two parties—if not one of friendship, at least one of nonaggression.

At the same time, we see that it was sealed in blood, as seen in the sacrifice that accompanied the covenantal oaths. The penalty for breaking the oath, for breaking the covenant, was made explicit in the sacrifice, for a covenant is more than just a promise. A promise is merely said, merely verbal, but a covenant is cut.

The actual terms used differ somewhat from what appears in our safe English translations. "The basic terminology describing the inauguration of a covenantal relationship vivifies the life-and-death intensity of the divine covenants. The phrase translated 'to make a covenant' in the Old Testament literally reads 'to cut a covenant'."[5] Thus, Laban proposed above, "Come now, let us cut a covenant, you and I." And we see at the end of the passage that Jacob did just that: he cut the sacrifice open and the covenant was inaugurated.

The meaning of the cutting, the sacrifice that signaled the initiation of a covenant, is that it is a graphic representation of the penalty for breaking the terms of the covenant. "The dismembered animals represent the

---

4. Gen. 31:44–54 NRSV.

5. Robertson, *Christ of the Covenants*, p. 8. As Robertson explains, this terminology of "cutting" a covenant permeates all of the Old Testament: Torah, Prophets, and Wisdom writings. He lists the following references in which covenants are "cut": The Torah, Gen. 15:18; 21:27, 32; 31:44; Exod. 23:32, 34; 24:8; 34:10, 12, 15, 17; Deut. 4:23; 5:2, 3; 7:2; 9:9; 29:1, 12, 14, 25, 29; 31:16; The Prophets, Josh. 9:6ff.; 24:25; Judg. 2:2; 1 Sam. 11:1, 2; 2 Sam. 3:12ff.; 1 Kgs. 5:12ff.; 2 Kgs. 7:15ff.; Isa. 28:15; 55:3; Jer. 11:10; 31:31ff.; Ezek. 17:13; Hos. 2:18; Hag. 2:5; Zech. 11:10; The Writings, Job 31:1; Ps. 50:5; 1 Chr. 11:3; 2 Chr. 6:11; Ezra 10:3; Neh. 9:8.

curse that the covenant-maker calls down on himself if he should violate the commitment which he has made."[6] Later when the people of Judah violated the terms of the covenant into which they had entered, God punished them in the manner in which the covenant had been cut.

> The men who have violated my covenant and have not fulfilled the terms of the covenant they made before me, I will treat like the calf they cut in two and then walked between its pieces. The leaders of Judah and Jerusalem, the court officials, the priests and all the people of the land who walked between the pieces of the calf, I will hand over to their enemies who seek their lives. Their dead bodies will become food for the birds of the air and the beasts of the earth.[7]

They had ratified the covenant by cutting a calf in half and passing between the halves; in the same manner they were rewarded because they had failed to keep that covenant. Similarly, if God were to ever break the covenant that he made with Abraham in Genesis 15, he would be ripped apart, as were the animals through which he passed. If this is impossible, then so is God's ever forgetting to keep his part of that covenant.

Laban and Jacob were bound by an oath of life and death that they would keep the terms of the covenant into which they entered. As Laban expressed it, the Lord himself would keep watch between them, the pillar would keep watch between them, and the pile of stones would keep watch between them. If either broke the covenant, the guilty party would be liable to the same fate as the sacrifice. It truly was a bond in blood; it was inaugurated in blood and it was punishable in like fashion.

Furthermore, according to Robertson's definition a covenant must be sovereignly administered. In most of the covenants of Scripture this means that it is given by God to humans. In the case of Jacob and Laban the fact that the covenant was handed down from above is evident from three complementary factors. First, it was to be overseen by God; he would be the judge between them if they broke the covenant, and it would be his job to exact punishment. Second, although Laban and Jacob made the covenant, it was binding also for their children and relations. We see that they were included in the sacrificial meal inaugurating the covenant. So far as can be seen from the text, this was not an eternal covenant. It did not continue through the generations after the two men died, but remains binding on them *and their relatives* for the extent of their lives.

6. Ibid., p. 10.
7. Jer. 34:18–20 NIV.

Thus, if Jacob's grandson were to transgress the terms while Jacob or Laban remained alive, that would call down on him the penalty just as if Jacob himself had broken the covenant. It was binding from the top down, or from its head, Jacob and Laban, to their heirs. This is more obvious in other covenants but is a constant feature.

Third, when Laban proposed the covenant, there was no haggling or bargaining. Laban set the terms for Jacob and he even set the terms for himself. At this point Jacob, who had spent the past twenty years dickering with Laban over stock and wages, did not bargain with him. They did not haggle over the exact boundary or over which terms would be acceptable. Haggling over prices was expected in the market place; for example, Abraham haggled (after a fashion) over the price of the land on which he buried Sarah. But never do we see any haggling over the terms of a covenant. The terms are stated and then ratified. Perhaps in a purely human covenant it would be possible to refuse to enter the covenant, yet even in these we do not find any haggling. Obviously, when God makes a covenant with people, he lays down the terms and there is no option of entering or not, or at least we never see anyone opting out of a covenant. People often fail to uphold their side of a covenant after they enter it, but that is another matter altogether.

Eve

Eve, the wife of Adam, was created as a covenant partner for Adam. Just as the covenant between God and Abraham and the covenant between Laban and Jacob were each initiated with the cutting of animals, the covenant of marriage was initiated by cutting Adam and removing a rib. That rib from which Eve was formed made her in fact one in body with her husband. Adam's response to meeting her was that "this at last is bone of my bones and flesh of my flesh."[8] We truly are all *adam*, for from Adam came even his own wife. Their children came from her, but she was exactly flesh formed from his own flesh, so the children came from him. Adam and Eve were "one flesh": they were both *adam*, and as such they were the prototype of all marriages.

But there is greater significance to the removal of the rib than just that they were one physically. We see that after removing the rib God "closed up its place with flesh."[9] The fact that it had to be closed up shows that God did not perform this removal by purely supernatural means; he

8. Gen. 2:23 NRSV.
9. Gen. 2:21 NRSV.

did not just wiggle his nose and the rib stopped being in Adam and began being outside of Adam. After its removal there was a real hole in Adam's side that needed filling and sealing. God healed the wound. But if there was a wound, then there was a cut or incision of some sort. The passage does not make clear how the cut or incision was made, but only that after it was made there was a hole in Adam. Adam was cut, and this cut resulted in the covenant of marriage.

In this cutting we see the trademark sign of a covenant. God had, of his own volition and without consulting Adam, cut a covenant. God had initiated the plurality of *adam*, which we saw hinted at in his numerically odd statements at Adam's creation. He now made *adam* two, yet they were one. And this one-dwelling-as-community was accomplished by God's cutting a covenant in Adam's own flesh. Adam's own body had become the sacrifice to put this covenant into effect.

The blessings of living in this covenant include the fulfillment and completion of the individual. To love a wife is to love one's own self; it is in fact to become more nearly whole, more fully human. "In this same way, husbands ought to love their wives as their own bodies. He who loves his wife loves himself."[10] Likewise, the penalty of violating this marriage covenant (which includes all forms of sexual sin, for sexual acts are covenant acts—either covenant making or covenant breaking acts) is in keeping with the mode of its inauguration; it also begins in the body of the covenant breaker. "For this reason God gave them over to degrading passions; for their women exchanged the natural function for that which is unnatural, and in the same way also the men abandoned the natural function of the woman and burned in their desire towards one another, men with men committing indecent acts and *receiving in their own persons* the due penalty of their error."[11]

It is to be noted that *adam* had become both one and two, and that *adam* was one and two of the same thing at the same time. In this there never has been a contradiction. *Adam*, that is, humanity, was fully manifested in Adam the man, and fully manifested in Eve, and fully manifested in the pair. That which Adam had been before his nap and God's surgery, he still was after, and Eve was just as much Adam as she was *adam*. They were one by her being formed from his rib, they were one by the marriage covenant, and they were meant to live as one in a manner that would reflect the mutually indwelling unity that characterizes the life of God.

---

10. Eph. 5:28 NIV.
11. Rom. 1:26–27, NASB; italics added.

Although we will not here consider all of the ramifications of the following statements, we may conclude from the preceding observations that the unity-in-diversity of Adam and Eve was set into place by a covenant and that this was in partial fulfillment of God's statement that he would make *adam* to express his own image. Therefore, there is no reason to see the unity-in-diversity within the Godhead as anything other than an eternal covenant between the Father, the Son, and the Spirit. Although we here arrive at this conclusion from a different angle, the same conclusion has been very ably defended in much greater detail by Ralph Smith in several books.[12]

Eve was created in a predefined relation to Adam just as Adam had been created in a predefined relationship with God. At the moment of creating the *adam*, God, by bringing humankind into being, created us already in relationship to himself, by making us to be his own image and living model. That relationship to God was never voluntary; Adam was never invited to come into relationship to God. He was created and made in it and for it. Eve, likewise, was never invited into a relationship with Adam. She had been made for just that purpose, and the relationship in fact preexisted her. Rather than fitting the relationship to her husband into her life, as if it were one aspect of her person, she was formed to fit the relationship. Adam had a need; he was incomplete without a partner; he could not express the image of God without a covenant partner. Built to fill that absence, Eve could not help but be in relation to Adam.

And that relation is a covenantal relationship.

> You flood the LORD's altar with tears. You weep and wail because he no longer pays attention to your offerings or accepts them with pleasure from your hands. You ask, "Why?" It is because the LORD is acting as the witness between you and the wife of your youth, because you have broken faith with her, though she is your partner, the wife of your marriage covenant.
>
> Has not the LORD made them one? In flesh and spirit they are his. And why one? Because he was seeking godly offspring. So guard yourself in your spirit, and do not break faith with the wife of your youth.
>
> "I hate divorce," says the LORD God of Israel.[13]

This short passage manages to include all that we have been contemplating. There is a covenant that binds the man and woman into a

---

12. Ralph A. Smith, *Paradox and Truth* (2002), *Eternal Covenant* (2003), *Trinity and Reality* (2004).

13. Mal. 2:13–16 NIV.

single unit and delineates their behavior. This covenant was instituted by God and placed onto the two people; he made them one. Likewise, God continues to guard the sanctity of this covenant and is quick to punish the offending parties; he is the witness between the man and his wife. And why did he place them into a covenant that makes the two one? Because he is one, and he wanted us, his offspring, to be like him. He dwells eternally in the unity of his covenant relationship. God's desire for us to be like him places an obligation on us to ardently guard ourselves from offending against this unifying covenant in which we live.

Only the penalty of blood is missing. It may be said, however, that standing in its place is the fact that God takes the side of the offended party and that he refuses to recognize the offender. God insists that his children be like himself, and he denies admittance to impostors who break faith in their marriage covenants. If a state of breaking faith is or becomes permanent, then the offender would be effectively disinherited by God. Such disinheriting or alienation applied also to those within Israel who broke his covenant: "Call him Lo-Ammi, for you are not my people, and I am not your God."[14]

The covenantal nature of marriage provides one of the most powerful and consistent images in the Old Testament. God himself places marriage in parallel to the covenant he has made with his people to be their God and for them to be his people. When they fall away from him and disgrace themselves with idols, he calls their unfaithfulness to him prostitution; they are his unfaithful wife. To break God's covenant is disgusting in the same way that it is disgusting for a wife to break covenant with her husband and prostitute herself on a street corner.

If one who broke a covenant sealed with the blood of a lamb was liable to being ripped open just as the lamb had been, then consider to what punishment the one who breaks a marriage covenant is liable. This covenant was sealed in the blood not of a lamb, but of a man. How much greater punishment hangs over the breaker of this greater covenant? And if that prospect is frightful, how much more terrible will be the fate of those who break the greater covenant sealed with the greater blood of Jesus Christ?

> Anyone who rejected the law of Moses died without mercy on the testimony of two or three witnesses. How much more severely do you think a man deserves to be punished who has trampled the Son of God under foot, who has treated as an unholy thing the

---

14. Hos. 1:9 NIV.

blood of the covenant that sanctified him, and who has insulted the Spirit of grace?[15]

"Casual" Covenants

We read in the second chapter of Genesis:

> For this reason a man will leave his father and mother and be united to his wife, and they will become one flesh.[16]

The unity of being that existed between Adam and Eve sprang both from their sharing Adam's body and from the covenantal bond that bound them together even more closely. That bond is reproduced within all marriages, and indeed we see in the New Testament that it is reproduced in the marriage bed, with or without the blessing of matrimony. For this reason Paul warns the Corinthians not to unite themselves with prostitutes.

> Do you not know that your bodies are members of Christ himself? Shall I then take the members of Christ and unite them with a prostitute? Never! Do you not know that he who unites himself with a prostitute is one with her in body? For it is said, "The two will become one flesh." But he who unites himself with the Lord is one with him in spirit.[17]

Even "casual" sex forms a bond between the participants that Paul describes in clearly covenantal terms, paralleling it with the covenant that unites us to Christ.

We can see, therefore, that the bond between a husband and wife is a fact about which they have little say. It is not a loose bond that can wax and wane with the changing desires or impulses of the two, but a bond written with indelible ink in God's own book. Whether we feel bound to each other or not, whether we realize it or not, our lives are bound up in the lives both of our covenant partners (wives and husbands) and even of our sexual partners; and by the unity engendered in the covenant that binds us to Jesus, he is made part of the mix. This is not to say that he is suddenly forced to save (to bind himself in a saving covenant with) all with whom any Christian is sexually involved. Rather, he is made, by the actions of his own people, the victim of their covenantal unfaithfulness just as are those with whom they inexcusably unite themselves.

15. Heb. 10:28–29 NIV.
16. Gen. 2:24 NIV.
17. 1 Cor. 6:15–17 NIV.

New Covenant

But marriage is a covenant between two humans, both fallible and both fallen. No matter how well meant the intentions of those who enter it, the result of the covenant is never a completely full and perfectly harmonious union. The covenant is never fully kept by its members. The new covenant of Jesus' blood, however, is of a different character from human covenants. Never will God's part of this covenant fail. Any breaking of this covenant will only be due to failure on our part. All that is promised on God's side will be fulfilled; we will be married to the monogamous Christ; together we will be his one bride. Thus, the covenant of Eve's creation and marriage finds its only possible fulfillment in the blood of Christ.

With the coming of Christ, suddenly a new world opens up. God has come to live with us; he says that he will remain with us until the end; he promises to live right within us. We now are told that we will become, together as a single unit, not individually, Jesus' bride.[18] We are summoned to a marriage feast that the Eternal Father is preparing for his only Son. We are summoned, but not as guests. We are summoned to appear dressed in white gowns, the bride around whom he has built a wall. We are warned to watch eagerly for the appearing of our bridegroom, to listen at the door for his approach, to keep plenty of oil in our lamps as we wait throughout the night.

A new covenant has been cut, but it is also a very old covenant. The Lamb was slain outside of Jerusalem to consecrate and inaugurate the covenant of our marriage to Jesus. We are now his bride, waiting to be taken in to the wedding feast at which our marriage will be consummated. We are now bound to Jesus just as Eve was bound to Adam. We are of one flesh with him; we intrinsically belong together. Jesus, our husband, will never fail at being the perfect husband to us.

He is also the Lamb slain before the foundation of the world; this covenant is both new and ancient. God has always planned for this marriage; it was to bring us into his family that he proposed that the whole Trinity work together to make us. This is the ultimate realization of the purpose for which we were created; marriage to God's Son is the ultimate fulfillment of the promise held out to us in the phrase "image of God."

Not only that, but Paul repeats time and again that it is also the new covenant that has finally united us to each other.

---

18. We are always referred to as the "bride" of Christ, never as the "brides" of Christ. Jesus is no polygamist. See, for instance, Isa. 62:5; John 3:29; Rev. 21:2, 9; 22:17.

> To me, the very least of all saints, this grace was given, to preach to the Gentiles the unfathomable riches of Christ, and to bring to light what is the administration of the mystery which for ages has been hidden in God, who created all things; in order that the manifold wisdom of God might now be made known through the church to the rulers and the authorities in the heavenly places.[19]
>
> Do not lie to one another, since you laid aside the old self with its *evil* practices, and have put on the new self who is being renewed to a true knowledge according to the image of the One who created him—a renewal in which there is no distinction between Greek and Jew, circumcised and uncircumcised, barbarian, Scythian, slave and freeman, but Christ is all, and in all.[20]
>
> Just as each of us has one body with many members, and these members do not all have the same function, so in Christ we who are many form one body, and each member belongs to all the others.[21]
>
> May the God who gives endurance and encouragement give you a spirit of unity among yourselves as you follow Christ Jesus, so that with one heart and mouth you may glorify the God and Father of our Lord Jesus Christ.[22]

That which the marriage covenant accomplishes for a man and a woman, the Jesus covenant accomplishes for all who belong to his family. And while most husbands and wives live in, at most, a partial fulfillment of their covenantal union, the Jesus covenant will finally truly unite us with each other in an ever increasing bond of love. We are being renewed in his image, and that image will not fade but will be perfected.

Enter the Trinity

First, the Holy Spirit has come as a covenant partner, to be united with us. Just as Eve was one with her husband and yet an individual, so also we are united to the Holy Spirit as he indwells us, even while we are yet on this earth. We are being brought not only into a covenantal unity with other humans, but even—what can scarcely be thought—with the Holy Trinity. Could any reader of Genesis 1:26, or any of the rest of the Old

---

19. Eph. 3:8–10 NASB.
20. Col. 3:9–11 NASB.
21. Rom. 12:4–5 NIV.
22. Rom. 15:5–6 NIV.

Testament, construe from it not only that we would become an image of the community of the Godhead, but also that we would actually *participate* in his life? Was it ever visible before the cross, before Jesus' promise of the Paraklete, before Pentecost, that we would be invited into the most exclusive fellowship imaginable?

No. Such communion was inconceivable until it became a reality. Before the present age it would have been considered blasphemy to suggest any such thing. The rulers would have said to us, "You, a mere man, have made yourself God."[23] But no such thing is the case. We are not to become God. We are to be united to him, but we will not be him. This unity with God does not change our ontology; we are and always will be human; we always will be *adam*; we never will become God. The understanding of indwelling expounded earlier makes it possible to envision a real unity that could exist between ourselves and the Godhead that in no way implies that we become gods. This unity is possible only through the new covenant that unites us to Jesus and through which he pours his Spirit into us and by which he has made our peace with God the Father. It is only through the cross that we are brought into that covenantal unity with our Maker that Jesus spoke of as "you in me and I in you and they in us."[24] We, being first united to Christ, will indwell the Father as Jesus indwells him and the Father will indwell us as he indwells Jesus. So also will we be united to the Spirit just as Jesus himself is.

When did God come up with that plan? If redemption were merely a return to Eden, then it would be enough to become united to each other in fulfillment of the covenant creation and marriage of Eve. If redemption is God's plan B, if it is his remedy for a bad start, then it is much greater than his original plan. Did he originally design us to remain in the garden and never to be brought into intimate communal fellowship with himself? Of course not. God understood his plan from the beginning; this was his "eternal purpose." The idea of God's making us to be his own image seems to proceed much further than anyone would have dared to guess. We were made not only to live a life of covenanted love *reflecting* Trinitarian individuality and unity, but also to *join into* the life of the Godhead.

But that presents us with a rather uncomfortable implication. God's original purpose in creating humanity did not just allow for the fall; it required it. If sin had not entered the world and enslaved us, Jesus could not have rescued us from sin on the cross. Then neither would we have become covenantally united to him through that cross. But without the

23. John 10:33 NLT.
24. See John 17:20–23.

union to God and the union to each other that were achieved by Jesus on the cross we could never fully become God's image. Sin was necessary to fulfill the design for which we were made.

How truly did Paul exclaim:

> Oh, the depth of the riches of the wisdom and knowledge of God!
> How unsearchable his judgments, and his paths beyond tracing out!
> "Who has known the mind of the Lord?
> Or who has been his counselor?"
> "Who has ever given to God,
> that God should repay him?"
> For from him and through him and to him are all things.
> To him be the glory forever! Amen.[25]

Likewise, it is the same new covenant that destroyed the dividing wall that separated Jew and Gentile, which made one new man.[26] The covenant at Sinai laid down strict guidelines to separate the Jews from the other nations; by that covenant the covenant-making God made them his chosen nation. They were not to eat as other nations ate; they were not to intermarry with other nations; and they were to follow strict rituals of cleanliness. These stipulations would serve to set them apart from the other nations and to make them into a holy people for their God. Now, in Jesus, God's own barrier was destroyed.

> For he himself is our peace, who has made the two one and has destroyed the barrier, the dividing wall of hostility, by abolishing in his flesh the law with its commandments and regulations. His purpose was to create in himself one new man out of the two, thus making peace, and in this one body to reconcile both of them to God through the cross, by which he put to death their hostility.[27]

Have we fully registered the expansiveness and depth of God's purpose? One new man. We have become a new *adam* sprung from the second Adam, enlivened by his sister, his bride, his Spirit. This new Eve, the Spirit of Christ whom he promised to his disciples before his death, has born a new race of *adam*, greater than the first. Just as the first Adam and Eve were physically and covenantally one, so are the second Adam and the Eve whom he has sent. Therefore, just as the first bore a race that was united both through the common birth and through the common covenant, so now is the body of Christ a unity manifested in a glorious

---

25. Rom. 11:33–36 NIV.
26. Eph. 2:14–15.
27. Eph. 2:14–16 NIV.

diversity through our common birth and common covenant, witnessed to in Ephesians 4:3–6: one body, one Spirit, one hope, one Lord, one faith, one baptism, one God and Father of all.

Adam's Covenant

As was seen in the chapter on the word "*adam*," the unity and diversity within humanity was implicit from the beginning in God's proposal to make us: "Let us make mankind in our image." We were made for the purpose of exhibiting, in creaturely form, the dynamic relationship that creates an actual and perfect unity from many individuals, yet that delights in the individuality of each and perfects each member's distinctiveness even while perfecting the union.

This relationship in God can be thought of as each individual's indwelling of each of the others, as Jesus referred to it in his prayer in John 17. We are made one with our spouses through a covenant that binds us together, and to be one experientially is to live in that covenant. To live as if not bound together is to be breakers of that covenant. Thus, the purpose of the marriage covenant is to frame the relationship through which we will begin to exhibit and experience, one to one, the infancy of a relationship like that which Jesus enjoys with his Father and with his Spirit.

But that is not to be the end of the matter; that is just the beginning. Jesus prayed that we all might be one just as he and his Father are one. And, let us repeat, that unity sprang from what Jesus referred to as "I in you and you in me." Trinitarian union springs from Trinitarian indwelling. We were never meant merely to unite with a single spouse, live in unity with that spouse, then die and rot separately. Rather, marriage seems to be intended to train us toward a greater end, toward fulfillment in a corporate life of indwelling such that we all would mirror the Trinity. Not that marriage is evil and therefore has no place in God's heavenly kingdom. Far from being an evil, marriage is a blessing conferred on our parents while they were still sinless. Even the blessing of living in God's Paradise was not fully "good" until it had been improved with marriage.

Rather than being an evil, marriage is a *blessed but minor* covenant that will be/has been superseded by a greater and more blessed covenant. It is a shadow that falls away in the face of the new and coming reality. The perfect unity attainable through marriage in the garden would still never have come close to the perfect unity with God and our fellow *adams* that is attainable only in Christ. This is why, although history began in a garden, it ends in a city.[28] The garden, even had we stayed there without eating the forbidden fruit, was itself only a shadow that must eventually fall away in face of the fulfillment of the image of God for which we were created. From the very foundation of the world it was intended that Jesus' prayer would be fulfilled.

> I ask not only on behalf of these, but also on behalf of those who will believe in me through their word, that they may all be one. As you, Father, are in me and I am in you, may they also be in us, so that the world may believe that you have sent me. The glory that you have given me I have given them, so that they may be one, as we are one, I in them and you in me, that they may become completely one, so that the world may know that you have sent me and have loved them even as you have loved me. Father, I desire that those also, whom you have given me, may be with me where I am, to see my glory, which you have given me because you loved me before the foundation of the world.[29]

Never had this prayer been fulfilled, although this relationship had from the beginning been the only life that could be called life. Aside from living within the covenant into which Adam had been made, into which Eve had been formed, into which their children were born, all else must be considered death. Even in Eden we do not see this covenant being fulfilled; consider the two parents' failure to look out for each other even before the fall. Adam did not protect his wife from the fruit, although he was standing beside her as she spoke with the serpent. Eve did not look to her husband for guidance but sought wisdom from the serpent over whom she was intended to rule.

It might be thought that these factors point to wickedness or evil in our first parents prior to their eating of the fruit. But the biblical record is consistent in placing the point of sin's entrance into humanity not before Eve's bite, but after. Sin had not entered the world in any lasting way by Eve's eating of the fruit. Rather, it was with Adam's eating, for death came through sin, but death came not through Eve but through Adam. Therefore, sin came through Adam, as Paul explains in the fifth chapter of Romans.

---

28. I wish I knew to whom, furthest back, this phrase should be attributed. The oldest form of it I have found is by Alexander Maclaren, who wrote, "Man's course begins in a garden, but it ends in a city," in his *Expositions of Holy Scripture: Second Timothy, Titus, Philemon, and Hebrews* (Grand Rapids: Baker Book House, 1977), p. 113.

29. John 17:20–24 NRSV.

But that leaves us with a bit of a problem. If our first parents were sinless until they had eaten the fruit, then how could they have chosen to eat the fruit, for surely that choice and all of the foolish steps leading up to it were sinful. Surely we must recognize a failure of character on the part of both Adam and Eve: Adam for not protecting his wife, Eve for not seeking her husband's guidance, both for listening to a teaching that contradicted their Creator's words.

However, that is to make too much of the state of our first parents; they were created pure, but not created perfect. They were as liable to failure and mistake as are any of our children. They were immature, not necessarily physically children (although there is no reason to suppose that they were not children, and there is every reason to believe that they were not flabby Europeans as they are sometimes portrayed in paintings), but naïve and unpredictable like children. They were not steadfast and certain of themselves, as our rarely realized ideal of an adult would want them to be. They were mutable, yes, liable to fall; but more than that, they were liable to foibles. And foibles are not necessarily sin. Their foolishness did not necessarily translate into sin that would cause a rift between themselves and their Creator until they had actually breached his direct command. Eve's foolish actions prior to actually eating the fruit cannot be thought of as sin, because no teaching of Scripture so characterizes them. Her eating was a sin; but it was a sin that touched on her alone, not that plunged all the rest of creation, and especially the whole human race, into bondage to sin and decay. Adam's eating did that.

But how was the sin of eating different from the sin of deciding to eat? What intrinsically differed between Adam's eating and Eve's eating?

The difference in each case is covenant. God had created Adam as a covenant creation, and had delineated the bounds of that covenant: Do not eat from the tree in the center of the garden. God had brought Adam into a relationship with himself in which strict requirements set the parameters. Adam would obey and God would be his God.

We notice that God had said beforehand why this human creation would be made. They would be his image; that was the role for which he created them. He had big plans for them. But he did not burden them with the full implications of that role immediately. Rather, he began by giving them a simple command, "Do not eat," and watching them fail in it. Had he expected them to keep the commandment? Of course not: he knew them too well. Then why did he give them a command that they would not keep? Did he just want to see them fall?

He did not maliciously desire to see them condemned; rather, "God has bound all men over to disobedience so that he may have mercy on them all."[30] He intentionally set us in a place from which we would fall, so that he could lift us up through the sacrifice of his Son. This was done, not so much with an eye to saving as many humans from hell as he possibly could have, but rather with an eye to glorifying his Son through giving him a great work to do. The Father entrusted the greatest work in all of eternity to his Son, life and death on Earth, and then raised him up and

> seated him at his right hand in the heavenly realms, far above all rule and authority, power and dominion, and every title that can be given, not only in the present age but also in the one to come. And God placed all things under his feet and appointed him to be head over everything for the church, which is his body, the fullness of him who fills everything in every way.[31]

It was for the sake of the Father's great love for his Son that all this great drama of creation, Eden, fall into sin, redemption, and final glorification of saints has been enacted. Even the damned in hell have played a part in the glorification of Jesus, so great is the Father's love of his Son. Just think how much thought, planning, and work went into this, not to mention the agony suffered by the Father as he was forced to turn away from his beloved Son. He did all of this to see his Son lifted high as a conqueror. This is the extent of the love that binds the Trinity together; this is the extent of the love that we must exert toward one another if we wish to think ourselves to be God's image.

Parallels

The parallels between the singularity and the plurality within the Godhead and the singularity and the plurality within *adam* are so all-encompassing that it is difficult to begin to list them as if there were a few points of contact. Rather there is an almost one-for-one mapping of the former onto the latter, with one major difference—but that difference so taints our perceptions and our experience of life and of our own humanity that the similarities may be overlooked despite their abundance. Therefore, let us recap a few of them in brief.

1. Both the Godhead and humanity are characterized by a real, intrinsic, and inescapable unity.

---

30. Rom. 11:32 NIV.
31. Eph. 1:20–23 NIV.

2. Both the Godhead and humanity are also characterized by a real and intrinsic individuality of persons.

3. The unity of the Godhead and the unity of humanity are each made perfect and complete in the bond of being covenanted each to the other.

4. Unity is expressed, exercised, and enjoyed by actively indwelling each other.

5. Neither we nor God are truly ourselves outside of these bonds of covenant, apart from active indwelling union with others.

The great difference that obscures these things is that while God is a covenant keeper, we are covenant breakers. While we are inescapably in a covenant relationship with all the rest of *adam*, we live as if we were not; we live as rebels to the bond and the potential glory for which we were made. We live in self-imposed exile from ourselves as well as from our God.

Although we are intrinsically bound together by a covenant too powerful to be evaded, we live as if we were independent and autonomous. Our very existence is dependent on a covenant that we do not acknowledge or fulfill. We are traitors to God, to humankind, and even to our very selves.

And yet, the covenant is not broken by our unfaithfulness to it.

> There is no such thing as a merely nominal Christian any more than we can find a man who is a nominal husband. There are many faithless husbands, but if a man is a husband at all, then he is as much a husband as a faithful one. He is a covenant breaker, but this is not the same as saying that he has no covenant to break.[32]

A husband who is unfaithful to his wife is vile, not because he has ceased to be a husband, but precisely because he is a husband. His unfaithfulness to his wife does not obliterate his responsibility toward her; rather, his responsibility exacerbates his guilt. He is rendered more guilty and worthy of contempt than he would have been had his relationship somehow ceased with his unfaithfulness. A survey of the references to Israel as an unfaithful wife and a prostitute shows that God chastised the Israelites not for negating his covenant but for living unfaithfully to it, for living outside of it while still being under it. Regardless of how unfaithful they were, they were an unfaithful wife precisely because they were still wedded to God. The covenant held regardless. Likewise, Paul speaks of those who

---

32. Douglas Wilson, *Reformed is Not Enough* (Moscow, Idaho: Canon Press, 2002), p. 96.

sin under the law and those who sin apart from the law. Those under the law remained under it regardless of breaking it; indeed, they were more guilty for just that reason.

Consider also the prodigal son. Could his faithlessness remove him from his father's heart or make him less of a son? He did not act like a son, but that had no effect on who he really was. He could remove himself from the home, but not from the family.

In just this way, humanity remains a covenant community even though we all live as though we were not. We lie and rob and cheat each other; we mock our friends behind their backs; we enslave nations and races; and we twist Scripture to condone our actions. In every way that we can think of, we set ourselves above our fellows. We live a life antithetical to the mutual indwelling covenant of love in which the Trinity dwells. But this living outside of the covenant does nothing to remove us from the covenant. We are still *adam*, still humanity, still our brother's keeper.

9

God's Image After the Fall

SIN is defined in the Westminster Shorter Catechism as "any want of conformity unto, or transgression of, the law of God."[1] This definition has served well for many years, but can it be improved?

In Romans chapter 5 Paul constructs a complex argument that concludes that there had to be a law before the Mosaic law.

> Therefore, just as sin came into the world through one man, and death came through sin, and so death spread to all because all have sinned—sin was indeed in the world before the law, but sin is not reckoned when there is no law. Yet death exercised dominion from Adam to Moses, even over those whose sins were not like the transgression of Adam, who is a type of the one who was to come.[2]

If sin is not reckoned where there is no law, then how could there be sin prior to Moses? Could death, the result of sin, reign without law? Not according to Paul. But sin was sin and death did reign. Therefore, before the Mosaic law there was already a law. But what was it?

Earlier Paul had taken pains to show that both Jews (with the Mosaic law) and Gentiles (without the Mosaic law) were sinners. In fact he had decided that Jewish sins were not fundamentally different from Gentile sins. He had summed up by saying that in regard to their redemption "there is no distinction, since all have sinned and fall short of the glory of God."[3] There is no distinction in their redemption because there is no distinction in their sin. The sin of neither is ultimately seen as a breach of any written code. All sin is seen here as falling short of God's glory. This verdict is the bottom line on sin.

But if falling short of God's glory is sin, then that implies that God's glory was our law or was the standard to which we were and are held and by which we are evaluated and judged. It implies that God's glory was the

---

1. *Westminster Shorter Catechism*, "Answer to Question 14."
2. Rom. 5:12–14 NRSV.
3. Rom. 3:22–23 NRSV.

law or standard for both those "under the law" and those "apart from the law." That makes God's glory a law or standard prior to and superior to the Mosaic law. And God's image, the requirement that we reflect his glory, is that law.

The fact that we have always lived under this obligation enables Paul to say that sin reigned even before the law, for God's purpose in creating humankind has never been rescinded. God's purpose for us continues to be that we should be a people for his glory, a people who are his image.

So sin could be defined as "any want of conformity unto, or transgression of, the law of God" as long as that law is not confined to any written code, but is understood as the precreation law of our purpose—to be the image of God. Therefore, I would amend the Westminster definition of sin to reflect this more basic understanding: Sin is any want of conformity to the image of God. This wording seems more closely to reflect Paul's understanding in Romans 3:23 and places us all squarely under sin, whether we are under Mosaic law or Christ's law or think ourselves to be under no law. In the terms we have used to describe the Trinity in the last two chapters, sin can be said to be a lack of full participation in the eternal intra-Trinitarian covenant of reciprocating love.

It can be argued that the law of God is complete in the great commandment, "You shall love the LORD your God with all your heart, and with all your soul, and with all your might."[4] True, if this commandment were kept then we would truly reflect God's image, for to love him is to walk as he walks and to live as he lives.[5] This greatest commandment is really an amplification of our duty to be his image, for what does it mean to love God except to think and feel about him and to act toward him just as he himself thinks and feels about himself and acts toward himself? To participate fully in the same covenant of love in which the Father, Son, and Spirit dwell is to fulfill the command to love God fully. In regard to what Jesus speaks of as the second commandment, what does it mean to love our neighbors except to think and feel about them and act toward them as their heavenly Father thinks, feels, and acts toward his neighbors?

Perfect keeping of these two great commandments, which constitutes conformity to his image, is righteousness. In future times, when all things will have been made new, the law as a legal code and the covenants will be swallowed up by the far surpassing joy of seeing him as he is and of truly

---

4. Deut. 6:5 NRSV.
5. See 1 John 2:6.

being like him.[6] The law is not our righteousness, but Jesus' name is "The LORD Our Righteousness."[7] If the law were or could be our righteousness, as the Westminster Shorter Catechism's definition of sin seems to imply, then it would be a temporary righteousness; but as it is, our eternal role will be to continually reflect God's glory, and he will be our eternal righteousness.

To say that Jesus is our righteousness and that keeping those two commands is righteousness is no contradiction. In the resurrection we will not need to keep the law *as law*, but will keep the law by nature because it is a distillation of who Jesus is. As we grow into the representation of his image, we will fulfill the Mosaic law, but not because it is law. Jesus did not struggle to live up to the law; the law struggles to express Jesus' character. A little boy does not exert himself at soccer practice in order to be fit, but for love of the game. As he does so, he becomes fit almost by accident. Similarly, Jesus kept the law almost by accident as he lived in love with his Father. He quoted the law to Satan, but he did not need to quote it to himself to keep himself from sinning.

Life and Death

When we fell, turning traitor against the Majesty whose ambassadors to creation we were, how ugly was that treason! What higher role could God have assigned to us than that of being a means to display all that God is? And how low have we fallen that we are now bound as slaves to God's first enemy! And not only bound, but also willingly remaining in Satan's service, against our rightful King and Husband.

Our fall is called death. When God threatened death "in the day that you eat,"[8] why did Adam live hundreds of years after eating? Was more in view in the word "death" than merely physical death? Expositors typically see death here as spiritual death, being primarily separation from God. Physical death or mortality is seen as a secondary meaning of God's warning and a secondary result of sin. And this is a reasonable interpretation, for our renewed communion with God is called "newness of life," "life from the dead," "life . . . abundantly" or "life to the full," and "life eternal."[9]

---

6. 1 John 3:2.

7. Jer. 23:6 NIV.

8. Gen. 2:17 NRSV.

9. For examples, see Rom. 6:4; Rom. 11:15; John 10:10; John 3:16, 6:40, 17:3; 1 John *passim*.

But why did God choose to use the words "life" and "death" for these spiritual states? Is he making an analogy that separation is like death and communion is like life? Or is there an ontological change beyond the relational change that took place at the fall? Of all of the models given for understanding God's image, only the one in which God's image is seen as our purpose and role in creation allows for more than an analogical reading of "life" and "death" throughout Scripture. Although it might be possible to argue that Adam and Eve were more beautiful or smarter before the fall, it cannot be argued that these traits are restored at regeneration. New life is not even a regaining of what these other models claim as our definitive pre-fall natures. But in fact, new life is more, not less, than a regaining of our pre-fallen state.

Purity could be said to be regained, at least Christ's purity is applied to us, but even so, calling purity "life" and the lack of purity "death" would be clearly metaphorical. A metaphorical understanding is acceptable as far as it goes, but if a nonmetaphorical understanding is equally plausible, then it should take precedence, although it does not necessarily deny the metaphor. For example, we could easily say that Nebuchadnezzar was a brute of a man, a wild beast. For most of his life this statement would, of course, be a metaphor; as such, it would be true. But for seven years it was more than a metaphor, and he was driven out to eat grass like the cattle. The metaphorical understanding, though still true, was surpassed by the literal. Or to say that someone is blinded by lust is normally to use the metaphor of blindness for the lack of judgment displayed by that person, but one evening in Sodom it became literally true. In these situations the nonmetaphoric understanding takes precedence over the metaphoric one without abolishing the truth of the metaphor.

As was said above, the understanding that we are made to be God's image and that this task is our role and God's motive for our creation, allows for a more simple understanding of the words "life" and "death." "Death is essentially separation. To die physically means separation from the land of the living, but not extinction. To die spiritually means to be separated from God."[10] These are the two typical understandings of the death to which Adam and his descendents were cursed in their fall, and both of these did result. But there was a more immediate type of death. Our separation from the land of the living and our separation from God (in terms of being driven from the garden of God, from the land in which they walked and talked face to face with God) do not result *directly* from our sin itself, but from God's *judgment* on our sin. But by the very act of

10. Gen. 2:17 NET, footnote.

sin we separated ourselves directly from our own reason for being. This death was immediate and did not wait for the judgment of God. We moved, by our own actions, from a life of fulfillment to a life of emptiness and vanity, a living death. This change was not the result of God's judgment per se, nor was it metaphorical, nor was it delayed. It was immediate both logically (directly entailed) and chronologically (happened at once). Our death consisted of being immediately separated from ourselves. We were now simultaneously God's image (our role never changed) and not God's image (our performance of this duty was rendered impossible).[11] We had been ripped apart at our seams, as individuals and as a race, in a way that we have never been able fully to comprehend. This internal and incomprehensible sundering was recapitulated by Jesus on the cross when he cried out, "My God, my God, why have you forsaken me?"[12] We have been ripped apart and God paid our penalty when he himself was incomprehensibly torn asunder on the cross. Consider how clearly Christ's suffering in our stead is presented in Isaiah 53:

> But he was wounded for our transgressions,
> crushed for our iniquities;
> upon him was the punishment that made us whole,
> and by his bruises we are healed.[13]

We are healed by his wounds—like for like. The punishment that made us whole, as we see in Jesus' words on the cross, was for Jesus/Father/Spirit to be rent asunder as we had been.

Truly he bore our sorrows and stood in our place. Our kinsman redeemer! What a God! What a savior!

As Soon as You Eat of It

Adam and Eve lived within the atmosphere of God's pleasure and their own fulfillment of their purpose in life. Life was not drab, but was utterly

---

11. Jesus especially—but also Paul and other biblical authors—clearly distinguishes spiritual death from physical death, and the spiritual is greater. Consider Jesus' statement that "the girl is not dead but sleeping" (Matt. 9:24, Mark 5:39, Luke 8:52). Was Jesus flippantly mocking the grieving of the family of the little girl, or did he see physical death as less than "real" death? When Jesus told a prospective disciple, "Let the dead bury their own dead" (Matt. 8:22, Luke 9:60), he surely did not expect corpses to rise up to dig graves. What could be the meaning of saying, "You were dead through the trespasses and sins in which you once lived" (Eph. 2:1–2), except that one can be alive physically yet dead spiritually?

12. Matt. 27:46; Mark 15:34 NIV.
13. Isa. 53:5 NRSV.

fulfilling. They were authentic, useful children of their heavenly Father. But as the saying goes, if you want to learn about water, don't ask a fish; ask a thirsty horse in the desert. Lacking any understanding of the possibility of being cut off from their inner peace, they were probably not fully conscious of the gloriousness of their situation, and they certainly had no conception of life outside of it. However, at the first taste of the fruit eaten in disobedience, the instant of death, they fell from all that they had known. For the rest of human history we have sought to put meaning into our lives; we have sought to find fulfillment; we have sought to grow by linking ourselves to causes larger than ourselves. We have sought to regain what we lost by that primal rebellion.

Note that we fell at the moment of eating. Our fall did not wait for God to walk in the garden and pronounce the curse on our ancestors. Immediately Adam and Eve were estranged from themselves ("and they realized they were naked"[14]); they were estranged from each other ("the woman you put here with me—she gave me some fruit from the tree"[15]); and they were estranged from their Creator ("and they hid from the LORD God among the trees of the garden"[16]). Suddenly each was seeking advantage over the other, each trying in vain to be God to the other. We can but little grasp the loss that occurred, for we have no familiarity with the blessedness of being at complete peace with ourselves, with each other, and with our God. All of these internal ramifications of the fall preceded God's coming down to the garden to curse (and to bless) us.

God's Image After the Fall

Was humankind still God's image after the fall? This is a most important question and it has been answered in many ways. The answers given always reflect differences concerning the meaning of "God's image" and concerning the real meaning and extent of sin as well as the anthropology and philosophy of the theologian.[17]

Martin Luther held that God's image was totally destroyed,[18] others that it was defaced. John Calvin said that it has been "vitiated and almost

---

14. Gen. 3:7 NIV.
15. Gen. 3:12 NIV.
16. Gen. 3:8 NIV.

17. Again, see the discussion by Karl Barth, *Church Dogmatics* (Edinburgh: T. & T. Clark, 1958), 3,1:192-94.

18. Martin Luther, *The Creation: A Commentary on the First Five Chapters of the Book of Genesis*, trans. H. Cole (Edinburgh: T. & T. Clark, 1858), p. 91: "Wherefore, when we

blotted out . . . confused, mutilated, and disease ridden."[19] These answers are based on the assumption that God's image is something implanted into humans, that it is an ability, characteristic, propensity, property, or desire. Had Luther understood God's image to be not a trait within us but God's purpose and role for humanity, then he never would have said that it was destroyed, for he knew that God's purpose in creation will stand. Given their assumptions concerning the content of God's image, however, different thinkers have been driven by other concerns in their theologies (especially the Reformed stress on the absolute slavery to sin into which humanity fell) to propose that we now live post-*imago Dei*, that the fall of Adam was the fall of God's image.

This proposal runs into a problem though, when we consider the only occasion between the Fall and the coming of Christ when God's image is referred to directly. In Genesis 9:6 God makes no distinction between Adam's having been in his image and the sinners of Noah's time and afterward.

> Whoever sheds the blood of a human,
>   by a human shall that person's blood be shed;
> for in his own image
>   God made humankind.[20]

These were post-Fall sinners whose lives God was protecting by saying that he considered them to be his image. These were those whom nearly every great theologian from Irenaeus to Augustine and from Aquinas to Luther has said are at best a mutilated image of God. But God says that, simply because he considers them to be his image, their lives are sacred and he requires that they be protected. All of the things that these theologians say of God's image—confused, mutilated, dead, diseased, almost annihilated, and so forth—are said in Scripture of humanity, but they are never said of God's image.

---

now attempt to speak of that image, we speak of a thing unknown; an image which we not only have never experienced, but the contrary to which we have experienced all our lives, and experience still. Of this image therefore all we now possess are the mere terms—the image of God! . . . But there was, in Adam, an illumined reason, a true knowledge of God and a will the most upright to love both God, and his neighbour"; quoted in D. J. A. Clines, "Humanity as the Image of God," http://www.shef.ac.uk/~biblst/Department/Staff//BibstResearch/DJACcurres/Postmodern2/Humanity.html.

19. John Calvin, *Institutes of the Christian Religion*, ed. John T. McNeill and trans. Ford Lewis Battles (Philadelphia: Westminster Press, 1960), pp. 188–90.

20. Gen. 9:6 NRSV.

Look also at the statement by James, "With [the tongue] we curse those who are made in the likeness of God."[21] Who could James be meaning by the word "those" if not the fallen race of sinners, and yet he says that they—or we—are still considered to be God's likeness.[22] These are the only two verses after the creation that refer directly to human beings as the image of God other than promises of a future fulfillment of that image. And there is in them no hint whatsoever that the image is either gone or diminished. Indeed, scanning through the uses of the word "image" in the New Testament (see the previous footnote for a few) makes clear that God's image is both in effect at present and awaits its fulfillment. Whatever we take this image and likeness to mean, we must guard against defining it in such a way that it no longer remains valid after the Fall. If it was neither destroyed nor mutilated at the fall, we are led to believe that the image must have its ground not in our nature but in the nature and character of God, for he alone is immutable. We are and remain God's image only because he created us as his image and continues to use us in this role.

Lifeblood

A closer look at God's command of capital punishment may help to clarify these distinctions.

> For your own lifeblood I will surely require a reckoning: from every animal I will require it and from human beings, each one for the blood of another, I will require a reckoning for human life.
> Whoever sheds the blood of a human,
> by a human shall that person's blood be shed;
> for in his own image
> God made humankind.[23]

God takes seriously the lives of the descendents of Adam, for they are made as his own image. That image did not cease with the fall nor with the death of Adam. We all are *adam* and were in Adam on that first day, and nothing we can do will ever remove us from the role into which we were created. As God's image our lives are sacred.

21. Jas. 3:9 NRSV.

22. The word James uses for "likeness" is εικων (*icon*), which is the same word used elsewhere to describe Jesus as the image of God (2 Cor. 4:4; Col. 1:15) and also the same word used in promising that we will be transformed into Jesus' image (Rom. 8:29; 1 Cor. 15:49; 2 Cor. 3:18; and Col. 3:10 [here "Creator"]).

23. Gen. 9:5–6 NRSV.

Why then did God not follow his own dictum and kill Cain when he confronted him with the murder of Abel? Surely if any murder required capital punishment it would be a murder committed simply for envy. But God did not put Cain to death; in fact, he marked him with a protective mark that probably saved his life.

Martin Luther notes importantly that "God does not inquire after sheep and cattle that have been slaughtered, but He does inquire after men that have been killed."[24] While we may ask why Cain was not executed by God for committing murder, we must also note that God did not ignore the deed but that in fact he did "require a reckoning." God confronted Cain with his sin and executed judgment, even if he did not execute Cain.

But though God prescribed death for murderers, yet he did not directly and immediately bring about the death of Cain. Did God fail to live up to his own standard? This riddle may prove easier to unravel if we first consider another riddle.

Unforgiven Blasphemy

Jesus warned those who disparaged his miracles that "any sin and blasphemy shall be forgiven men, but blasphemy against the Spirit shall not be forgiven. And whoever shall speak a word against the Son of Man, it shall be forgiven him; but whoever shall speak against the Holy Spirit, it shall not be forgiven him, either in this age, or in the age to come."[25] This passage is a source of much contention, often being linked with a couple similar warnings in Hebrews,[26] and most of the discussion centers around what exactly the sin that will not be forgiven entails. Let us leave that question aside and focus on another aspect of the puzzle: Why is Jesus unwilling to forgive such blasphemy?

We know that he is unwilling, not unable, for he says specifically that such sin "shall not" rather than "cannot" be forgiven. Judgment and mercy are in his scepter;[27] the right to judge is his alone;[28] he holds "all authority in heaven and on earth."[29] He will have mercy on whom he will

---

24. *Luther's Works*, vol. 1, *Lectures on Genesis, Chapters 1–5*, ed. Jaroslav Pelikan and trans. George V. Schick (Saint Louis: Concordia Publishing House, 1958), p. 285.

25. Matt. 12:31–32 NASB.

26. See Hebrews 6:4–6; 10:26–27.

27. Rev. 19:15.

28. John 5:22–23.

29. Matt. 28:18 NIV.

have mercy, and he says that he will have none on those who blaspheme the Holy Spirit. His blood is sufficient for such forgiveness; his death is payment enough for such a sin. But his sovereign decision is that his blood will not cover that sin; his death will not pay for it. He has retained to himself the right to wreak vengeance where he will, and he declares that his vengeance will be felt by those who blaspheme his Spirit.

For our present purposes we need not let ourselves get dragged into controversies over what exactly this blasphemy of the Holy Spirit is; it is enough to know that it is an offence against the third member of the Trinity, against God the Spirit. Jesus is protective of his Spirit, of his Father's Spirit, just as a man is protective of his new bride. The lover says to his beloved, "You are a garden locked up, my sister, my bride; you are a spring enclosed, a sealed fountain."[30] Jesus' Spirit, his sister, his bride, is his sealed fountain, his enclosed spring, his locked-up garden into which he will allow no trespass. He will not allow this bride to be trampled. Of all the sins of the world that Jesus bore on the cross, he did not bear, he would not bear, this sin against his beloved Spirit. As Jesus suffered for the sins of the world, he did not suffer for sin as a generic fact, but he suffered for specific sins and in the place of specific sinners. He did not just bear sin; he bore my sin and my sins. And of all of the sins that he willingly bore, there is one that he refused to bear, one that his Father did not ask him to bear, and that is the offence that Jesus calls blasphemy against the Holy Spirit.

Does a man protect his bride? That is the merest shadow of how Jesus protects his Spirit. Let someone threaten a man's wife or his children and all caution will be flung to the wind as he seeks by any means to ensure their safety. Jesus will endure any pain on our behalf, on behalf of his future bride, but he will not endure attacks on his current bride, his sister, his garden locked up.

A side note must here be clarified, for we have referred to the Holy Spirit as Jesus' bride and also to the church as Jesus' bride. Jesus is no polygamist. The church is often called the bride of Christ; the Holy Spirit is not. The term "bride" is used of the Spirit here to emphasize the protective stance that Jesus bears toward his Spirit, so like that spoken of in the Song of Solomon. It is interesting, however, that the church is not united to Jesus as his bride until it has first been united to his Spirit. First the Holy Spirit is sent by Jesus to dwell in us and to establish what Paul calls "the unity of the Spirit."[31] Only as a single body united to his Spirit are we

30. Song 4:12 NIV.
31. Eph. 4:3 NRSV.

presented to Jesus as his bride. Perhaps the idea of the Holy Spirit as Jesus' bride is more than figurative.

But there is more here than the mere analogy of marriage. A man and his wife become one flesh; Jesus and his Spirit are one.

Jesus' adoration of his Spirit caused some confusion among his disciples. "It is for your good that I am going away. Unless I go away, the Counselor will not come to you; but if I go, I will send him to you."[32] How could it be for their good that Jesus would leave them? the disciples wondered. But Jesus so adored his sister, his Spirit, that he knew any friend of his would likewise be enthralled by her.[33] The Jesus whom we hear in the New Testament is madly in love with his Spirit and he is jealously protective of her. He exhibits toward his Spirit the ideal of how a man should feel and behave toward his wife. She is precious and delicate, requiring and being worthy of his utmost care.

Ephesians 5:25–32 compares the love and care of a man for his wife to the way in which Jesus loves and cares for his church. This is profoundly true, but we must realize that Jesus did not turn over a new leaf when he came to Earth; he did not become self-giving for the first time in Bethlehem. He lived on Earth the same life and displayed the same character that was and is his from everlasting to everlasting. And he gave himself on our behalf just as he eternally gives himself for his revered Father and his beloved Spirit. Paul's doctrine of husbandly care of wives could just as easily have been derived from Jesus' care for his Spirit as it was from his care for his church, but Paul undoubtedly chose the analogy that fell nearer the experience of his hearers.

Jesus as Our Example

Paul's exhortation to husbandly care in Ephesians comes in a passage that makes it clear that we are to treat not only our wives with such diligent concern, but also all others with whom we come into contact. Children are to behave toward their parents with careful attention to the honor of the parents, while parents are to seek the emotional well-being of their children, not merely external obedience. Slaves and masters are to behave

---

32. John 16:7 NIV.

33. I am not here advocating goddess worship or the idea that we should speak of the "Motherhood" of God rather than the "Fatherhood" of God. I do not pray to "Our heavenly Mother," and neither should you. I am merely borrowing the relationship expressed in Song of Solomon and applying it to Jesus and his beloved Spirit, for the type of love and the ardor expressed seem to mirror the tender affection and self-sacrificing love that Jesus has for his Spirit.

God's Image After the Fall

toward each other for their mutual edification, neither of them abusing their positions but using the position into which God has placed them to build the other up.

In short, we are all exhorted by Paul to follow Jesus' example of strenuously working toward the betterment of others, toward the increased honor of others. Just as Jesus was willing to suffer on the behalf of his people, as he also strove to do his Father's work for the honor of his Father,[34] as he set aside his own glory to glorify his Father and the Holy Spirit, so also we are to behave in all of our relationships.

Paul exhorts us to live our lives in a manner that imitates the mutually self-sacrificing covenant of love that we see lived out by the Trinity. He is, in fact, restating and expanding the creation commandment that we are to be God's image. If we were made to be God's image, then we should live as he lives, as they live. Our life as a people, and our lives as individuals, should be lived in imitation of the straining toward each other and intense self-sacrifice that make the three one. We too must strain to consider others as better than ourselves, and to do unto others as we would have them do unto us, and to love our neighbors as ourselves.[35] To really follow such commands would be to emulate the covenant that unifies the Trinity, that which makes God God.

So, going back to consider the question of why God did not kill Cain, we begin to see a possible reason. Could it be that the duty of killing Cain lay with human government rather than with God? Could it be that as God's image, it is our responsibility to protect our own just as Jesus protects his Spirit? Could it be that we as a people must take on the role of husband toward each of our members, in this way beginning to live out the life that the Trinity lives, beginning to express the love that makes the three one and will make all of God's children one? Is capital punishment love?

We remember that Jesus refuses to forgive those who commit the sin that he calls "blasphemy against the Holy Spirit." This is a much more permanent death that he is guaranteeing to those who offend his beloved than that which we could mete out to a murderer. Yet it is undeniably motivated by love. It is motivated, certainly, by wrath against those who have offended the Holy Spirit, but that wrath springs from Jesus' love for his Spirit. The covenant of mutual love between the figures of the Trinity is the basis of Jesus' wrath.

---

34. See for example John 5:17–40, 14:10, and Jesus' prayer in chapter 17.
35. See Phil. 2:3; Luke 6:31; and Luke 10:27.

Could the built-in covenant of unity among all who are *adam* be the basis for leaving capital punishment to human means? The phrase, "For in his own image God made humankind," is often taken as referring to the reason for executing the murderer. But that is not the way the command is given. Let's look at the verse again:

> Whoever sheds the blood of a human,
> > by a human shall that person's blood be shed;
> for in his own image
> > God made humankind.[36]

The fact of our being God's image is given not in explanation of the need for capital punishment for capital crimes; rather it is given in explanation of the need for that sentence to be carried out *by human hands*. The murderer shall be killed "by a human." God has his role, but so do people.

Why is the execution of judgment left to human means? Is this so that we can wreak vengeance on our enemies? Are we here commanded to usurp the place of him who said, "It is mine to avenge; I will repay"?[37]

Might it not rather be that we are to execute judgment as an act of love toward the murdered person in loyalty to the knowledge that we are our brother's keepers? If we treat as a light thing and choose to overlook a murder, is that in any way respectful of the one who was the victim? Does not love require that we exact the full penalty, even if the murdered person would likely not seek a harsh sentence on her own behalf?

Indubitably the Holy Spirit would be willing to apply the blood of Jesus' sacrifice to cleanse from sin those who had committed the blasphemy that Jesus refused to forgive. It was in fact an offence against the Holy Spirit, and for the Spirit not to forgive it would have been out of keeping with the commandments that are given to mere mortals; how much more would the God of the universe keep his own commandments. But it is not the Holy Spirit who said that he would not forgive such a blasphemy; Jesus refused.

If we imitate Jesus, if we follow the life pattern that we learn from God, then we too will refuse forgiveness in certain circumstances. This is foreign ground to most Christians, but I repeat that we must refuse to forgive, that is, refuse to overlook, some sins. To fail to follow Christ in this point is to turn our backs on those in the fellowship of *adam* who no longer have a voice with which to forgive.

36. Gen. 9:6 NRSV.
37. Deut. 32:35 NIV.

Does this mean that we hate the murderer and joyfully slaughter him? Absolutely not, though "his commands are not burdensome,"[38] and we will be able to rejoice in the love shown to the murderer's victim and to the unity of all humanity. It is a remarkable thing that we do exact judgment in favor of those who are not present to plead their case to the court. It is a Christ-like, loving act.

But, someone will argue, if we are to seek Trinity-imitating unity with all people, then how are we expected to kill other people? Is this not a contradiction?

This is an important question. Again we must refer to the actions of God to see wherein the distinction lies. God the Father sent his Son into the world because he loved the world, so that the world would be saved through the Son.[39] He even sent his Son to Capernaum, resulting in the salvation of some few and the increased condemnation of many others.[40] Did the Father's love for those who were perishing stop him from sending his Son to them? On the contrary, his great love for those whom he was saving caused him to send his Son, while the others who obstinately removed themselves from his love have their blood on their own hands. Likewise, murderers have by the act of murder irreversibly removed themselves from unity in the bond of love with the individual whom they have killed. There is no chance of being reconciled to their victim on this earth.

Does this mean that murderers are damned without any hope of obtaining mercy when they plead for it? By no means. Rather, the command that murderers be executed by human hands is given to humans and not to God. God can and does pardon many murderers, and many will live in joyful union in his Kingdom who have forfeited the opportunity to live so here. There is no constraint on God in this commandment; he remains free to show mercy where he chooses to show mercy. The constraint of human justice and the freedom of divine justice and mercy are not to be set at odds.

Nevertheless, we see that the murderer has irreversibly removed himself from any chance of working toward unity with the victim of his sin, yet we continue to be bound to the victim by the covenantal union that exists between us. That covenantal obligation is not constrained by life or death, by time or distance, by race, color, or creed. We are bound up with all *adam*, with all humankind. That covenantal union is part of the created

---

38. 1 John 5:3 NIV.
39. John 3:16–17.
40. Matt. 11:23–24.

order and it is not in our hands either to accept or to reject it. It exists as surely as we ourselves exist.

But it remains in our hands to live in or to live outside of that covenant. To murder is to make permanent (so far as permanency is at the disposal of the murderer, although ultimately it is not) a rejection of the covenant that binds murderer and victim. We who seek to remain within the covenant are bound to apply justice to the one who has offended against the unity of the covenant. In this way we follow God's commandment and follow Jesus' example.

10

Jesus, God's Express Image

Let us leave Adam and Eve and consider instead the new Adam, that new man, the image of the invisible God whom God the Father sent as his representative and ambassador (mediator). If we have concentrated in this text more on the union that makes one *adam* of many individual humans, it is because that is the more neglected doctrine, and the one more closely tied to the creation story that we are studying, not because it is more important than our union with Jesus. In reality, the final union of humanity in one *adam* is possible only through our prior individual union with Jesus.

When we consider Jesus in his deity, we understand him to be co-eternal with the Father and the Spirit, sharing power and knowledge and judgment. The three are in eternal relationship, interaction, and agreement.

In considering him as human, we realize that he suffered hunger, weariness, and even temptation, just as we do. But even as we affirm these truths of Jesus' humanness, do we not often feel as if his deity outweighed his humanity? We are comfortable, are we not, with the notion that although he occasionally "acts human," such as weeping or being ignorant of the date of his own return, he is much more fully God? Did he not spend most of his time doing things that we could never do?

Jesus did many miracles that are beyond our unaided potential, but his greatest achievement, the one that made it possible for him to bear our sin and assured that death could not hold him, is the one that gets the least attention: his life. We know that Jesus was tempted just as we are, yet without sin. And his sinlessness reached deeper than just being free from sins of commission; he never committed a sin of omission. He never failed to turn the other cheek. He never forgot to love his enemies or to beg mercy for (not from) those who were nailing him to the cross. He showed himself to be truly in the character of our Father in heaven.[1]

---

1. See Matt. 5:45.

In all ways Jesus showed us the Father. In the way that Jesus searched for and found the lost sheep, we see the Father's deep concern for his wandering flock. In Jesus' choice of companions, ignorant dirty fishermen, treacherous tax collectors, whores, and lepers, we see the Father's choice. Jesus said, "The Son can do nothing on his own, but only what he sees the Father doing; for whatever the Father does, the Son does likewise."[2] And in that most quoted of verses, "For God so loved the world . . . ," John tells us that in Jesus we see an expression of the Father's love for us.[3]

Paul summed up this part of the role that Jesus fulfilled when he called him "the image of God."[4] To what exactly was Paul referring? Was it only to the fact that Jesus was the invisible made visible, that Jesus was the "exact representation" of God,[5] that Jesus was, in fact, God in flesh so we could see him? In such passages, this nuance seems to be part of what Paul has in mind. But Paul's choice of phrases also takes us back to the creation. Paul is quoting from the Septuagint translation of Genesis 1:26 and 27, but with a distinction. Jesus *is* the εικων (*icon*) while we are never said to *be* the εικων, but always to be created *in* or *as* or *for* the εικων. Paul so emphasizes that Jesus *is* God's image that we might almost be inclined to wonder whether the statement in Genesis 1:26 might refer only to Jesus, just as the promised "seed" deliverer of Genesis 3:15 had reference, not to all of Eve's seed, but only to Jesus, the Seed.[6]

How does the Greek word εικων (*icon*) relate to the Hebrew words that are generally translated as "image" and "likeness?" Interestingly, εικων seems to encompass the meanings of both words and more. In Hebrew the צלם (*tselem*, image) usually bears a physical resemblance to the thing it represents and always functions symbolically as a stand-in for the original, while the דמות (*demuth*, likeness) bears a resemblance to the original on any of a wide variety of levels. In a similar manner, the εικων both resembles the original on some level and also serves as more than a stand-in for it. "In the New Testament the original is always present in the image. What is depicted is here given visible manifestation."[7] The author of the letter to the Hebrews juxtaposes the "shadow" of the law with the

2. John 5:19 NRSV.
3. John 3:16.
4. 2 Cor. 4:4 NIV; see also Col. 1:15.
5. Heb. 1:3 NIV.
6. Gen. 3:15; Gal. 3:16–18.
7. Gerhard von Rad, Gerhard Kittel, and Herman Kleinknecht, "εικον," in *Theological Dictionary of the New Testament*, edited by Gerhard Kittel (Grand Rapids: Eerdmans, 1964), 2:395.

"realities" (εικονα, *icona*) which were to come.⁸ These "realities" represent a real manifestation; the author is comparing the shadow to the unveiling of the real thing. That real thing is the εικονα. And in Romans 1:23 people exchanged the glory of God for representations of the εικον of things created. "The distinctiveness of the expression lies in the juxtaposition of ομοιωμα [*omoiōma*], which here means the copy, and εικων, which is the original copied, *i.e.*, the thing itself and its form."⁹ Thus the word εικων encompasses all that is contained within the Hebrew צֶלֶם (image) and דְּמוּת (likeness), expressing an even closer affinity for the thing represented than both Hebrew words together seem to require. So for Paul to use the Greek εικων precludes any need for him to fill it out as in Genesis 1:26 with a gloss, for the force of the gloss is included in the one word.

Jesus is the perfect humanity and full image we were all made to be. He has succeeded in fulfilling the task for which we were all created. He has perfectly reflected the glory of his Father. As our elder brother he has preceded us in this attainment, "so that he might come to have first place in everything."¹⁰

So the reference to Jesus as the "image of God" is simultaneously a reference to his deity and to his humanity. In fact, in this phrase we become aware that Jesus was, in a sense, more human than any of the rest of us. In the fall we lost the ability to grow into the role for which we were created, the role that in fact makes us human. We became less than fully human by our sin. The context mandates that we understand that Jesus not only was expected to reflect his Father but actually did so, while we have failed to live up to our role. Jesus lived the human life as it was always supposed to be lived, as God's perfect image. "Behold, the man!"¹¹

For this reason Jesus is referred to as the "last Adam."¹² He is the fountainhead of a real humanity, a real people who will become the fulfillment of God's desire to form his image, of which the first Adam was only a shadowy anticipation.¹³

---

8. Heb. 10:1.
9. Rad, Kittel, and Kleinknecht, "εικον," in Kittel, *TDNT*, 2:395.
10. Col. 1:15–18 NRSV.
11. John 19:5 ESV.
12. 1 Cor. 15:45 NIV.
13. See Rom. 5:14.

Conformed to His Image

If God's image is understood to be our role in creation, death will be understood primarily as separation between our commission and our achievement. We were made to reflect God's glory, and to fail is to die. If this is so, then new life, real life, eternal life, abundant life must be the uniting of our role and our achievement.

How can we who are dead be brought to life? Paul answers, "If, because of the one man's trespass, death exercised dominion through that one, much more surely will those who receive the abundance of grace and the free gift of righteousness exercise dominion in life through the one man, Jesus Christ."[14] When we are given the gift of righteousness we will begin to "exercise dominion in life." But what is righteousness, and what is trespass? If our purpose is to reflect God, then trespass is to wander from this purpose and righteousness is to live in this purpose. Trespass is death and righteousness is life. When Paul says "Present yourselves to God as those who have been brought from death to life, and present your members to God as instruments of righteousness,"[15] he is not saying to do two things—first, present yourselves to God, and second, present your members to God—but rather he is using parallelism to say one thing: that our new life is lived in righteousness before God and that righteousness is found in living the new life. They are one and the same thing. Righteousness is not found merely in *being* but also in *doing*.

And Jesus is our righteousness.[16] Reformed theology typically accentuates the objective, while downplaying the subjective in the Christian life. The fact that Jesus is our righteousness is seen as meaning that his righteousness has been reckoned to us in a legal fashion. We are admonished to look to his finished work on our behalf and to the life that he lived in our place.

But did Jesus live so beautifully just to perform a legal substitution of giving us credit for having lived his life with him? Jesus came as "the image of God"[17] to raise the bar visibly back up to where it had always been. In his life, not only lacking in sin but also full of good works, we see what it means to live as God's image. Jesus did fulfill the Mosaic law in our behalf, but he also fulfilled the prior law or standard, which had been put in place before the creation of Adam: to be God's mirror. And Paul goes on to say

14. Rom. 5:17 NRSV.
15. Rom. 6:13 NRSV.
16. Jer. 33:15; 1 Cor. 1:30.
17. 2 Cor. 4:4 NIV.

that we see "the light of the knowledge of the glory of God in the face of Jesus Christ."[18] As we look to him, in his living face, "seeing the glory of the Lord as though reflected in a mirror, [we] are being transformed into the same image."[19]

God's declaration made before our creation is reiterated when we are told that God has predestined some "to be conformed to the image of his Son."[20] God himself is seeing to it that his plans for Adam's race will be fulfilled. He will continue until he has brought us into conformity to his Son's image, which is his own image.

There are many "you are / you must" parallels in Scripture, such as "once you were darkness, but now in the Lord you are light. Live as children of light."[21] You are light / you must live as light. While we are being conformed to Jesus' image by God's power and plan, we must simultaneously strive to become conformed to the same image. "And just as we have borne the image of the man of dust, let us also bear the image of the man of heaven."[22] You are being conformed / be conformed. And to be conformed we look to Jesus not only as the legal warrant for our redemption, but also as the pattern by which we model our lives.

God's eternal purpose has never changed. We are now to model and reflect God just as Adam was to have modeled and reflected God. But now Christ has become our new exemplar, the εικων to which we must be conformed, superseding the old covenant law. "By this we may be sure that we are in him: whoever says, 'I abide in him,' ought to walk just as he walked."[23] Just as Adam needed no weighty law, for he walked with the original whom he was to imitate, so also we who are now in Christ have outgrown the old law and walk again with the original.[24] Imitate him.

As we imitate him we know that he is walking beside us all the way. He said, "Take my yoke upon you, and learn from me."[25] A yoke is a device that binds two animals together so that they are working and pulling together as one animal. We are to walk beside Jesus and learn to pull just as he pulls, so that together with him we work not as two, but as one.

18. 2 Cor. 4:6 NRSV.
19. 2 Cor. 3:18 NRSV.
20. Rom. 8:29 NRSV.
21. Eph. 5:8 NRSV.
22. 1 Cor. 15:49 NET.
23. 1 John 2:5–6 NRSV.
24. The superiority of Christ to the law is a recurrent theme in the New Testament, e.g., Gal. 2:15-21 and Heb. 7–10.
25. Matt. 11:29 NRSV.

Conformity to the image of Christ, the image of God, is also an already / not yet phenomenon. "This means that it now is, and yet that it is still to be. It is enjoyed, but not yet enjoyed. Its eschatology is even now at work, and its presence has an eschatological basis."[26] In being both already and not yet, conformity to Christ closely parallels the already and not yet structure of salvation: we were saved (by the eternal decree), we were saved effectually (on the day we were made alive in Christ), we have been saved (by Jesus on the cross one Friday outside Jerusalem), we are being saved (through progressive sanctification), we are now saved (secure from destruction), and we will be saved (on that final day). So also we were conceived and ordained to be God's image (by his eternal decree), we were created to be God's image (on the sixth day), we have become his image (united to Christ through his cross and thus becoming his body), we are being conformed to the image of Christ (through progressive sanctification), we are now his image (in our role as created humans, and even more in our role as newly re-created children of God), and we will be conformed to his image (when we at last see him as he is).

To God—Father, Son, and Holy Spirit—be glory forever and ever. Amen.

No Exit

Jean Paul Sartre, in *No Exit*, his famous play depicting life in hell, describes a room with three people, one man and two women. The room is nicely furnished and there is nothing untidy or discomforting at all in the room. In fact, it is a very cozy little drawing room in which these three will spend eternity. But this is hell; they are not here to enjoy the coziness of the room, but to suffer eternally for their sins. The punishment is not in the room, but in the company. The man wants to think in peace and quiet while one woman needs to jabber incessantly at him to drown out the thoughts in her head. The other woman, meanwhile, lusts incessantly after the talkative woman, but the talkative woman only wants the man to acknowledge her, which he refuses to do. Round and round, in increasingly miserable and hopeless cycles the depth of alienation and loathing increases to sink them ever lower into the despair of the hell in which they are trapped.

For Sartre, hell is other people. And this may be; perhaps hell is being eternally trapped in a room with Jean Paul Sartre.

---

26. Rad, Kittel, and Kleinknecht, "εικον," in Kittel, *TDNT*, 2:397.

The biblical vision of heaven, it seems to me, is also other people, but a very different kind of people, and a very different kind of self that is brought into this heaven. This vision of heaven, however, is more difficult for many today to cling to than is Sartre's vision of hell.

An Impossible Dream

I have walked now more than a decade, nearly one third of my life, with Jesus. Yet even now I resonate with Sartre's antisocial vision; what Scripture says about the coming kingdom I see only as a far distant and almost unreal hope. Nevertheless, on that mist of a hope I stake my life, for all else is death.

When I was a child, maybe six or seven years old, my family and I ate dinner at the cabin of the great naturalist, Richard C. Davids. After dinner, while we all enjoyed ice cream (I had chocolate but Mr. Davids had vanilla for he said that chocolate ice cream would freeze his mouth and give him a headache), Mr. Davids showed us the birds eating on a feeder at his window. He explained to me that he was color-blind, that although he could see clearly, he could not distinguish one color from another. He could name the colors of the birds in his feeder, but he could neither see those colors nor visualize what they must look like. I realized that although he could name the colors, he did not know them.

As we left for home that evening, I thought long and hard about the idea of being color-blind. I could see the colors and I could tell him what color something was, but he could never understand what that color was. Only someone who sees colors would understand what I meant when I described something as red. Then I began to wonder if other people saw red the same way that I did. Is red the same for everybody? How could we know? We all know that an apple is red, so what we see when we look at an apple we all name as red. But does it look the same for other people? The only way that I could think of to describe the color was to name other things that are also red. But I realized that such a method would not even begin to answer the question, for they also would have learned to name the colors just as I had, but that would not mean that what they saw looked the same to them.

That evening I came to understand that no one else could know or understand anything that I thought or said; they could only interpret what I said or did by their own experiences and their own understandings. I realized that no other person would ever be able to know me, just me, from inside my own understanding. No one would ever be able to hear me. Not really. That night I became alone.

From that evening on, I am sure that I have never lived a moment without the knowledge of my utter earthly isolation working somewhere in my mind and tinting every other thought and damping every relationship. On this earth I know myself to be alone. What I think and feel, God and I know. No one else can. And I can never really understand anyone else, either. There is an impenetrable wall between us.

This is not how we were created to experience life. As God's image, we were created to experience life as he experiences life. And God is an eternal community dwelling with and in and through each other, knowing each other intimately. Elohim said, "Let us make." And they are making. They will succeed. They will finish what they started. We will be *adam*.

History

In light of the doctrine of God's image as it is presented in the preceding chapters, the meaning of history can be summed up as follows.

God the Father set his mind to glorify his beloved Son and to celebrate the wonder of the love that binds together the Father, the Son, and the Holy Spirit. To this end he formed a plan to establish something called *adam*, something that would be defined by its resemblance to the Godhead and would live as they live. *Adam* would be *adam* by the same power that God is God. That power that makes God to be God is exercised in the radical covenant of indwelling love and the resultant unity that make the three one. Just such a life and power would be at work in *adam*, such that they would become one as he and his Son and his Spirit are one.

His plan, of necessity, required the co-working of all three persons who are the one God. At its outset he called for the work to be a unanimous effort of all three with words to the effect of, "Let us work together to make humanity so that it may be our image, and for the purpose of being our likeness." In love, some of the details of his plan he kept to himself, not telling them even to his Son. These he held in reserve to be revealed at the proper time. Thus, Jesus participated in his Father's plan in faith and trust and obedience, because it was his greatest desire to honor his Father by being a co-worker with him.

This majestic work of making *adam* is taking place in three distinct stages, each of which requires the participation of each member of the Trinity. There was a first creation in which the Father called for each element to be created; his Son brought forth these elements; the Spirit put life into the elements and sustained them through the course of history. Eve was born of Adam's blood, by breaking his flesh, and the Holy Spirit breathed into her life. In this way, humanity was perpetually bound together by a covenant that makes them all intrinsically a single unit. But this intrinsic unity did not satisfy the Father's purpose.

At creation *adam* was childlike and immature, not yet grown into the likeness of its maker. In this childlike state, *adam* rebelled against God and became a miserable creature at war with its creator and with each other, and each individual member of *adam* was even at war with itself. This rebellion itself was part of the Father's plan, for he did not want *adam* to grow to maturity and develop into the likeness of the Trinity while remaining in some measure aloof from its maker. Indeed, the rebellion was necessary in order to facilitate the next two stages of lifting humanity into its high position, by which two stages the Father meant to magnify the worth of his Son and put his own love for his Son on display.

Then there was a second creation, in which we again see the three working together to further the Father's goals. The Father sent his Son to earth to become an *adam*, a human. As such, Jesus was absolutely the fulfillment of his Father's words; Jesus was the very image and likeness of the Godhead. As such he was the first full realization of what his Father had proposed that they make. God would then have been justified in annihilating the rest of humanity and casting all other children of Adam and Eve into a pit of fire for eternity were it not that he had other goals and had made other promises. But the Father desired above all to lift up for adoration this Son whom he loved so. Simultaneously, he desired to bring with his Son many other sons and daughters to be a bride, bathed and dressed in wedding garments, made fit for his Son. For these reasons he sent Jesus to the cross.

On the cross Jesus bore his Father's wrath toward us as it was poured out on him, reconciling us to our creator. He sealed the covenant that bound us to himself in what we will ultimately come to recognize as a marriage covenant, and he made new the covenant that binds together the splintered fragments of humanity into a single unit. He was a new Adam and in him was born a new humanity, a new *adam*. This new humanity is where the Father will ultimately fulfill the image of the Trinity. Uniting us first to his Spirit, the Father is creating a new humanity, born of Jesus' blood, his broken flesh, and his Spirit's inbreathed life, who will together become the bride of Jesus. Once again, the Father calls for the elements by name, the Son creates them, and the Spirit gives them life and sustenance.

There is yet to come a third stage in the creation of this *adam* that is to be the image and likeness of the Trinity. We are not yet, even washed with Jesus' blood and indwelt with his Spirit, the fulfillment of the Father's plan. Bound though we are by covenant to his Son, and by both the covenant of Eve and the covenant of Jesus to one another, we yet remain covenant breakers.

A day is coming when the bride of Christ will be brought *en masse* into the house of Jesus' Father, dressed in new robes, and ushered into a banquet hall to celebrate our marriage feast. At that time we will finally and fully become like him, we will finally see him as he really is, and we will begin to live the life of love that characterizes God himself. We will then live our life as he lives his life and we will join the Trinity and live with them the fulfilled covenant of love as sons and daughters of the Father and as the bride of Christ.

That day is not the end: it is the beginning of life; it is the beginning of *adam*. For eternity we will join the Holy Spirit in searching the depths of the God the Father's heart. We will give ourselves to and for each other. We will be caught up and swept away in the exuberant delight that Jesus has in his Spirit. We will eagerly open our hearts to those around us, and never will our trust be abused. And never will we come to the end of these pursuits, for just as the heart of God has no limit so also we will find that the heart of our neighbor is endless in its delights and profoundly engaging. Never will it be heard in that day, "Oh, I already understand that man. He is no longer interesting." Rather, "we will have eternity to get to know the infinite,"[27] and the longer we are there the greater will be our delight in all that we find. Our parents "knew that they were naked and were ashamed," but we will know and be known without embarrassment and without limit.

Then will God the Father look at the fulfillment of his plan, the image of the Trinity, and the adoring bride of his Son, and he will be satisfied.

L'Chaim, To Life!

Jesus is preparing us to experience what it really means to be human, what it really means to live. We will live in and with and through each other; we will love as we have never loved; we will search out the deep things of each other and will love the persons that we find in those deep places. We will give ourselves away and will take freely of each other, not from selfishness,

---

27. This is a saying of my good friend, Greg Meyer.

but from a desire to understand how best to know, to serve, and to love that other one.

We will no longer be alone. We will no longer be alone. We will no longer be alone.

We will know ourselves through the eyes of others, and those others will love us and will search us with loving minds. We will have no more secrets, no more dread of discovery, no more hiding behind false images. Instead we will give ourselves away to each and every other. Never will we run out, but always have more to give. Even while we reach out to others to know and to love them, they will be reaching out to us. I will seek only for the best for my neighbor with no thought for myself, but my own needs will not go unattended; others will make it their joy to tend not only to my needs but also to my comfort. I will be loved by a community who will care for me with deeper passion than I now attempt to care for myself. I will be freed from self-attentiveness, because others will be attentive to me. They will see and seek to see more of me; they will search out the deep things of me; they will listen with their hearts and minds, eagerly bent toward deepening their love to me.

And we will look back, if we do look back, on this present thing we call life, but which Scripture calls a death-in-life, and we will see that it was no life at all. No life, but only a scraping around the edges of life, searching, searching, always searching for something that will satisfy. In this life, except for special moments of clarity, we insatiably long to fill ourselves: with fun, with learning, with fame, with children, with wealth, with anything that will finally satisfy the emptiness we feel. From our future perspective this thing that we now call life will look like what it is: a groveling in the dust searching for clods of dirt to take to our hearts and give us meaning.

But then we will have Christ, we will have his body which is us, we will have a life that flows out from ourselves and into one another even while their life is flowing into us. We will take no thought for our own welfare, but will seek for the welfare of every other. Others will be fulfilled in us and we in them and all in Christ and Christ in his Father and in his Spirit and they in him. We will be built up together to the full standing of the building, to the completion of the city, to the eternal increasing of his government and his peace. Never will there come a day when the limit has been reached and there is no higher up to climb or further in to go. In that eternal day it will be our passion and our joy, our labor and our love, to penetrate each other and the heart of our God, and to seek new revelations of glory there through which we may find new honors to heap on each other and onto God.

Then we will know what it is to live. Then we will know what it is to be *adam*. We will live life as God lives his life and we will finally be his image.

And we will live. Really live. Together. Forever.

L'Chaim, to life!

Bibliography

Aquinas, Thomas. *Summa Theologica*. Translated by the Fathers of the English Dominican Province. London: Burns Oates & Washbourne, 1922.
Arminius, James. "Disputation XXVI, On the Creation of Man After the Image of God." In *The Works of James Arminius*. www.ccel.org/arminius/works2.html.
The Articles of the Synod of Dort. Edited and translated by Thomas Scott. Utica, N.Y.: William Williams, 1831.
Baker, Douglas P. "The Image of God: According to Their Kinds." *Reformation and Revival Journal* 12, no. 2 (Spring 2003): 97–109.
———. Review of *Eternal Covenant* and *Paradox and Truth*, by Ralph A. Smith. *Christianity and Society* 14, no. 2 (April 2004): 29–30.
Barth, Karl, *Church Dogmatics*. Vol. 3, pt. 1, *The Doctrine of Creation*. Edinburgh: T. & T. Clark, 1958.
Berkouwer, G. C. *Man: The Image of God*. Translated by Dirk W. Jellema. Grand Rapids: Eerdmans, 1962.
Bowman, Robert M. "My God, How Great Thou Art, Sermon for the Transfiguration." Sermon delivered at United Catholic Church, Melbourne, Fla., March 7–8, 1998. www.rmbowman.com/catholic/s980307h.htm.
Bulgakov, Sergey Nikolayevich. "Die Christliche Anthropologie." In *Kirche, Staat und Mensch. Russisch-orthodoxe Studiën*, pp. 209–55. Geneva: Forschungsabteilung des Oekumenischen rates für praktisches christentum, 1937. Quoted in Berkouwer, *Man: The Image of God*, p. 49.
Calvin, John. *Institutes of the Christian Religion*. Edited by John T. McNeill and translated by Ford Lewis Battles. Philadelphia: Westminster Press, 1960.
Catechism of the Catholic Church, Doctrines 1704, 1705, 1706. www.vatican.va/archive/ccc_css/archive/catechism/p3s1c1a1.htm.
Cochrane, Arthur C., ed. *Reformed Confessions of the 16th Century*. Philadelphia: Westminster Press [1966].
Edwards, Jonathan. *The Freedom of the Will*. Morgan, Pa.: Soli Deo Gloria Publications, 1996.
Epstein, I., ed. *The Babylonian Talmud: Seder Nezikin*. Vol. 3, *Sanhedrin*. Translated by Jacob Shachter and H. Freedman. London: Soncino Press, 1935.
Erickson, Millard J. *God in Three Persons: A Contemporary Interpretation of the Trinity*. Grand Rapids: Baker, 1995. Quoted in Smith, *Truth and Paradox*, pp. 48–49.
Finney, Charles. "Affections and Emotions of God." *The Oberlin Evangelist* (October 9, 1839): 169–70.
———. "Where Sin Occurs, God Can Not Wisely Prevent." *The Oberlin Evangelist* (August 2, 1854).
Hebrew-English Tanakh. Philadelphia: Jewish Publication Society, 1999.
Heidelberg Catechism. In Cochrane, *Reformed Confessions of the 16th Century*, pp. 305–31.
Hoeksema, Herman. *Reformed Dogmatics*. Grand Rapids: Reformed Free Publishing Association, 1966.

Bibliography

Jenni, Ernst, and Claus Westermann. *Theological Lexicon of the Old Testament.* Translated by Mark E. Biddle. 2 vols. Peabody, Mass.: Hendrickson Publishers, 1997.
Jewish Virtual Library. www.jewishvirtuallibrary.org.
Jónsson, Gunnlaugur A. *The Image of God: Genesis 1:26–28 in a Century of Research.* Stockholm: Almqvist & Wiksell International, 1988.
Keach, Benjamin. *Tropologia, A Key to Open Scripture Metaphors.* London: Printed by J.R. and J.D. for E. Prosser, 1682.
Kittel, Gerhard, ed. *Theological Dictionary of the New Testament [TDNT].* Translated and edited by Geoffrey W. Bromiley. 10 vols. Grand Rapids: Eerdmans, 1964–76.
Kleinknecht, H., and W. Gutbrod. "νομοσ." In Kittel, *TDNT,* 4:1022–91.
Kuyper, Abraham. "Dictaten Dogmatiek." Translated in Herman Hoeksema, *Reformed Dogmatics,* pp. 295–96, and quoted in Smith, *Paradox and Truth,* pp. 74, 78.
———. *The Work of the Holy Spirit.* Translated by Henri De Vries. Grand Rapids: Eerdmans, 1979.
Kuyper, Abraham, Jr. *Het Beeld Gods* (1929). Quoted in Berkouwer, *Man: The Image of God,* p. 39.
Lenormant, François. *The Beginnings of History According to the Bible and the Traditions of the Oriental Peoples, From the Creation of Man to the Deluge.* New York: Charles Scribner's Sons, 1882.
Lewis, C. S. *The Lion, the Witch, and the Wardrobe.* New York: HarperCollins, 1978.
Lockshin, Martin I. *Rabbi Samuel Ben Meir's Commentary on "Genesis": An Annotated Translation.* Lewiston, N.Y.: Edwin Mellen, 1989.
Luther, Martin. *The Creation: A Commentary on the First Five Chapters of the Book of Genesis.* Translated by H. Cole. Edinburgh: T. & T. Clark, 1858. Quoted in D. J. A. Clines. "Humanity as the Image of God." http://www.shef.ac.uk/~biblst/Department/Staff//BibstResearch/DJACcurres/Postmodern2/Humanity.html.
———. *Luther's Works.* Vol. 1, *Lectures on Genesis, Chapters 1–5.* Edited by Jaroslav Pelikan and translated by George V. Schick. Saint Louis: Concordia Publishing House, 1958.
Maclaren, Alexander. *Expositions of Holy Scripture: Second Timothy, Titus, Philemon, and Hebrews.* Grand Rapids: Baker Book House, 1977.
Mars Hill Audio. *Tacit Knowing, Truthful Knowing: The Life and Thought of Michael Polanyi.* MP3 CD. Charlottesville, Va.: Mars Hill Audio, 1999.
Martin, Lee. *A Dictionary of Special and Technical Terms for Hebrew and Greek Studies.* http//earth.vol.com/~lmartin/HBGKDICT.HTM.
Orr, James. *God's Image in Man* (1948). Quoted in Berkouwer, *Man: The Image of God,* p. 40.
Pasco, Allan H. *Allusion: A Literary Graft.* Toronto: Univ. of Toronto Press, 1994.
Polanyi, Michael. *The Tacit Dimension.* New York: Anchor Books, 1967.
Rad, Gerhard von, Gerhard Kittel, and Hermann Kleinknecht. "εικον." In Kittel, *TDNT,* 2:381–97.
Robertson, O. Palmer. *The Christ of the Covenants.* Philipsburg, N.J.: Presbyterian and Reformed, 1980.
Sayers, Dorothy. *The Mind of the Maker.* San Francisco: Harper Collins, 1979.
Shakespeare, William. *Hamlet.* New York: Washington Square Press, 1992.
Skinner, John. *A Critical and Exegetical Commentary on Genesis.* New York: Charles Scribner's Sons, 1925.
Smith, Ralph A. *Eternal Covenant: How the Trinity Reshapes Covenant Theology.* Moscow, Idaho: Canon Press, 2003.

Bibliography

———. *Paradox and Truth: Rethinking Van Til on the Trinity by Comparing Van Til, Plantinga, and Kuyper*. Moscow, Idaho: Canon Press, 2002.

———. *Trinity and Reality: An Introduction to the Christian Faith*. Moscow, Idaho: Canon Press, 2004.

Van Til, Cornelius. *An Introduction to Systematic Theology*. Philipsburg, N.J.: Presbyterian and Reformed, 1978. Quoted in Smith, *Paradox and Truth*, p. 41.

Verkhowsky, Serge. "Die Lehre von Menschen im Lichte der orthodoxen Theologie." *Evangelische Theologie*, 11 (1951–52): 310–23. Quoted in Berkouwer, *Man: The Image of God*, p. 50.

Wenham, Gordon J. *Word Biblical Commentary*. Vol. 1, *Genesis 1–15*. Waco, Tex.: Word Books, 1987.

Wesley, John. *John Wesley's Notes*. www.ccel.org/w/wesley/notes/.

Westminster Shorter Catechism. www.reformed.org/documents/WSC_frames.html.

Wilson, Douglas. *Reformed Is Not Enough*. Moscow, Idaho: Canon Press, 2002.

www.ingramcontent.com/pod-product-compliance
Lightning Source LLC
Chambersburg PA
CBHW072144160426
43197CB00012B/2242